Living in color!

Get started on a perfect palette for your home that suits your lifestyle and personality.

Decorating a home that reflects who you are begins with color. Yet for most of us, making color choices can be daunting. Paint displays offer thousands of hues, fabrics beckon in myriad patterns, and suddenly, basic beige looks safe and easy. That's where we can help. We've consulted the experts, gathered the images, and provided basic steps to help you select your best colors for a room or your whole house.

At the beginning, "Color Inspiration" gives you clues on where to look for your muse and how to pull a palette from an object you love. Next, "Color Mood & Meaning" explores how color ties to your emotions and personality. Then, our room-by-room guide, "Using Color in Rooms," shows you galleries of gorgeous palettes. If you're color shy, we give you step-by-step color confidence in "Add Color in Stages." For those looking for a unified scheme for the house, we cover that in "Color Through the House." Color basics and hands-on advice in our "Color Workroom" section take you from theory to practice.

Give yourself the time to explore this book and see where your imagination and creative juices take you. You'll love the journey.

Gayle

Gayle Goodson Butler,
editor in chief

Top tools for your tote

Journal to make notes and jot down measurements and product information.

Fine-point pen that won't bleed or smear.

Fan deck from your go-to paint source.

Small scissors to snip fabric and trim samples.

Multitool pocket knife with a flat-head screwdriver to open paint cans.

Digital camera to capture an inspiring color combination.

Home decorating apps such as a paint color matcher. Then test your palette at *BHG.com/color-finder* before you choose samples.

Clear project file to view project plans and hold collected samples.

Adhesive lint roller to remove fabric swatch threads.

contents

decorating with
Shells

Bring your love of the ocean
indoors with these fun and
whimsical seashell-inspired
items for the home

1

4

7

8

color inspiration

Find out how to hone in on the color
choices that reflect your passions, your
personality, and your lifestyle.

getting started

A little inspiration goes a long way. Try our designers' ideas to spark your color creativity and find the fresh palette that's right for you.

Q: How do I overcome my color commitment phobia?

A: Ask yourself these questions: What is your favorite color? What colors do you dislike? When you think of a color, what memories or feelings come to mind? What colors do you find yourself wearing over and over?

—**Kelly Keiser,** interior designer

Q: What has inspired you to select a room color in the past?

A: I just painted my living room an earthy pink. I spent a month in India and saw this color everywhere—on buildings, in stone, worn by people. Inspiration sources include travel, books, and magazines, just seeing what's out there in the world. Look at nature and how colors all work together in a garden or in a bunch of wildflowers on the side of the road. Take chances and try different things. See what feels good to you.

—**John Loecke,** interior designer

Play with paint chips!

Q: I've found my inspiration piece. Now what do I do?

A: Pinpoint which color in the inspiration piece grabs you first, then build from there. Don't worry about exact matches. Play around. For example, a burgundy color in an inspiration piece could translate into dark brown. Don't get hung up on paint names, either. They're just labels.

—**Patrice Bevans,** interior designer

Q&A

Q: How do I know a color is right for my room?
A: Let the idea go that there is one "right" color or you may fail to recognize some very beautiful possibilities for a space. Many colors you think are wrong simply create a different effect.

KELLY BERG
INTERIOR DESIGNER

EDITOR'S TIP
Basic office or school supplies, such as a sketchbook, a photo album, an expanding file, or a zippered pencil bag, can be a big help as you try to keep all your little pieces of inspiration together and carry them with you for constant reference and revision.

In the mood

If you're in a color quandary, don't wait for ideas. It's time to go out and get them.

Designer tool.
Make a mood board. This is where you see what you're drawn to and how everything fits.

Hunt and gather.
Grab, photograph, or tear out anything that catches your eye. It's all grist for your creative mill.

Evolving eye.
Tack up your treasures on a board. You'll notice your color and style tendencies start to emerge.

Play around.
Pin up crazy combos—you might be surprised by how many of them really work.

"Find the ideal color in a treasured collectible. If it's your favorite color, use it as an accent so you appreciate it more. In small splashes, it remains special."

—**Melissa Gurney,** interior designer

BLUE POINTS
Dashes of turquoise dot the room, thereby maintaining the color's rare gemlike quality. Caramel walls bathe the room in warmth.

FAVORED SHADE
above right A treasured carriage clock sparked the turquoise, brown, caramel, and cream color palette in the living and dining rooms.

BOOK NOOK
above, far right Flowing cream silk draperies define a reading alcove. Ceramic Chinese garden stools provide flexible seating while supplying satisfying bursts of vivid turquoise.

BLUE DOG GROUP
right Turquoise antique Foo Dogs caper on the hearth and mantel. Painting your walls and trim in subdued neutrals will provide a canvas for colorful collections, especially a single-hue set such as these.

UNITED FRONT
below right Touches of pink unify the adjacent living and dining rooms, as do the matching turquoise lamps and brown shades. The upper wall color deepens in the dining room to a dark chocolate brown, infusing the space with a cozy feeling.

Q&A

Q: How do I use my color choices in a room?
A: Use each color at least twice. Repeat your wall color in the form of pillows or other accents to unify your theme.

DEE SCHLOTTER
COLOR EXPERT FOR
PITTSBURGH PAINTS

Benjamin Moore
Cambridge Heights

Pacific Palisades

Jupiter Glow

Middlebury Brown

Dune White

look around you

When you're out and about, keep your eyes peeled for pleasing color combos you can adapt for your decor.

PRODUCE PICK
below and right Color palettes show up in unlikely places. The farmer's market or produce aisle at the grocer is a cornucopia of color. Shades of fruits and vegetables inspired the mix of hues that energize this living room.

DESTINATION COLOR
above and right Bring home the relaxing atmosphere of a vacation or favorite view with a color scheme inspired by your travels. This watery blue, cloudy gray, and sandy beige palette was suggested by a majestic view on a secluded beach.

Choose your colors in the room for which they're intended and in the same position they'll eventually occupy. Look at wall color chips vertically, and never against a white wall. Instead, hold them next to furniture that will be in the room. Select flooring or rug colors on a horizontal plane. Drape fabric samples over a piece of furniture.

THINK SMALL

above and left **If you've decided on a color, look for an object (such as this bird votive) that captures the feeling you want to create. Take your decorating cues from the colors and style of your inspiration object. Here, different shades of purple and brown bring interest and variety to the color palette and balance the warm and cool hues. A touch of harmonious coral pink pumps up the color volume.**

Orangery

Cinder Rose

Pelt

Farrow & Ball
Calluna

Brassica

follow your passion

Let the personal choices you've already made—your wardrobe, china, works of art—influence color selections for your rooms as well.

CLOTHING CUES
below and right **This vibrant mix of colors and patterns came out of the closet to inform a blooming bedroom palette. The bold striped curtain panels pull hues from favorite garments, while the blossoms on the duvet cover sparkle with jewelry hues. If a dress or skirt inspires a wall shade, your paint store can use that piece to create an exact color match.**

GET THE DISH
above and left **While you wouldn't choose your china based on a wall color, you can find a perfect color combo for a room in the shades of a china or dishware pattern. The body color of these cups provided the hue for sunny kitchen cabinets. Accent colors are pulled from the pretty band of flowers.**

Q&A

Q: I have several favorite colors. How do I choose from them?
A: Since you seldom start with an empty room, begin with something there you love or are sentimental about. Use it as a springboard for a color palette.

JOSEPH BOEHM
SENIOR INTERIOR DESIGNER
BETTER HOMES AND GARDENS®

ARTISTIC ENDEAVOR

above and right **Draw inspiration from a piece of art. It can cue your color scheme and suggest a style. The simplicity of this artistic composition is reflected in the clean lines of the living room furnishings and accessories. The painting's dominant green hue is used as an accent color rather than for the walls, which could have overwhelmed the space.**

echo the past

If you're drawn to the styles and furnishings of a different era, let the retro color combos guide your choice of palette.

FRESH INDULGENCE
right and below **Find your muse in a vintage vase filled with colorful blossoms. This carefree blend shows off the joys of tradition with a twist: Dazzling orange and chartreuse roses unexpectedly pair with fuchsia daisies to offer the same sort of visual surprise as the paisley wall coexisting with a classic quilt.**

THAT '70S HUE
left and above **Infuse personality into your space with retro colors inspired by the style of your favorite decade. Bright blocks of earthy hues recall the shades popular in the 1970s. Start with bedding to guide other choices: A sheet set in solid neutrals and one in a bright color can be mixed and matched. Top with a solid-color quilt and bold, patterned shams.**

When working with vintage elements, a neutral backdrop gives you license to mix with abandon an array of colors and patterns that are held together by theme.

PILLOW PASSION

above and left **If you appreciate the midcentury aesthetic of keeping things streamlined and colorful, set a white sofa against a white wall as the canvas for pops of color and indulge your passion with pillows. You can get your style fix from vintage pieces, scraps, and secondhand fabrics sewn into pillow covers. Swap them out easily if your style or color preferences change.**

color mood
& meaning

Explore what color can say about you,
and see how to group these revealing hues
to create a personal palette.

sapphire
Heat up too-cold rooms by showcasing this jewel tone on painted wainscots, patterned pillows, and upholstery fabrics.

powder blue
Accentuate this ethereal tint with crisp white woodwork, dark wood finishes, and pearlescent and silver accessories.

aquamarine
This warm-water hue promotes relaxation and conversation, so put it center stage in living rooms and entertaining areas.

cobalt
This powerful tone rules on painted floors, solid-surfacing countertops, and awning-striped fabrics. Pair it with mustard yellow for a dynamic scheme.

cerulean
Heavenly blue creates drama when highlighted on painted or papered walls, cabinet finishes, and glass-tile treatments.

blue

Comfortable as a pair of well-worn jeans, this striking spectrum includes a wealth of sea-to-sky shades, gemstone colors, and deep twilight tones.

denim
The true-blue hue suggests truth, constancy, sincerity, and orderliness.

baby blue
Delightfully delicate, this peacefully pale blue promotes tranquillity.

sky blue
This fountain-of-youth shade makes rooms appear fresh-faced, playful, and energetic.

navy blue
The room-warming tone represents authority and stimulates smart thinking.

robin's egg
A happy-go-lucky and soothing color, this hue carries the promise of spring.

turquoise
The cool gemstone color creates calming spaces and helps room occupants focus their thoughts.

Color strategies. REFRESHING FAVORITE.
Globally favored, blue universally pleases because of its reassuringly familiar associations, its calming properties, and its versatility. **MODERATE TEMPERATURES.** Using icy shades or too many blues can make rooms feel cold. Warm things up with a ceiling painted gold, orange, or red, or introduce warm hues with rugs, artwork, and fabric flourishes. **CREATE COHESION.** Weave blue through every room. Pile flowery pillows on sofas; hang country-checked kitchen valances; dress bedrooms in toile; and paint bathrooms aqua to forge perfect unions from front door to back. **ENHANCE VIEWS.** Complement blue with natural nuances such as grassy greens, sandy beiges, cloudy whites, and woody tones.

easy, breezy blue

> "Denim is a great color option for upholstery fabric because it wears like blue jeans. And what color doesn't look good with jeans?"
>
> –**Cortney Singleton,** interior designer

Q&A

Q: **There are so many shades and tints of blues. How do I choose which one to paint my room?**
A: Ask at the paint store about a color's light reflective value (LRV). The higher the LRV, the more light will bounce around the room. A lower LRV color will absorb light, making a room seem moody.

KELLY BERG
INTERIOR DESIGNER

DIGGING DENIM
above left **An arresting juxtaposition of casual and elegant elements, this handsome room hosts family-friendly and sophisticated dining experiences. The drapery panels' deep indigo bands darken the denim blue of the kicky slipcovers, made dressier with embroidered medallions.**

CONTEMPORARY COMPOSITION
above **Reddish-blues deepening toward purple fabulously complement cool turquoise patterns on walls and floors. The gray love seat and gold-upholstered bench provide visual relief, while the patterned carpet, throw pillow, and artwork show off the room's diverse shades of blue.**

PERFECT PARTNERS
opposite **Blue and white create simply striking rooms that always buoy spirits. Introduce the high-contrast color combo via wallpaper, coverlets, fabrics, and furniture pieces. Soften its impact with midtone wood finishes, pearl-gray accent walls, and sage accessories.**

Style setters

Use blues to expand your palette and enhance your home's style.

Caribbean warmth. Combine indigo blues with terra-cotta, pink, and lively greens and yellows to create tropical character.

Refined settings. Promote classic comfort with slate-blue walls, green velvet upholstery, gold accent fabrics, and red-toned wood pieces.

Garden fresh. Brighten bedrooms and baths with cornflower blues, rosy pinks, sunny yellows, and leaf greens.

Seaside scheme. Fashion "life's a beach" scenes with aquamarine walls, seashore motifs, and awning-striped fabrics.

teal
Casually combine this watery hue with Caribbean colors or accent it with almond and brown for more elegant environs.

"Paint finish can impact the mood of blues. Chalky flat finishes are warm, while shiny blues will give a bit of chill."
–**Stephanie Hoppen,** author of *Choosing Blue: Color You Can Live With*

peacock
This intimate, concentrated color looks even better when paired with cream woodwork and citron accessories.

azure
Though bold, this hue is still soothing. Try it in a room that needs focused energy, such as a home office.

aqua
Use this tone to dress up a flea market find or as a soothing counterweight to brighter green-tinted blues.

French blue
Redolent of the French countryside and the Côte d'Azur, this shade brings continental sophistication to any room. Pair it with yellow accents for a classic scheme.

SPACE SAVVY

above right **Slate blue unites vanity, wainscot, and windows to visually stretch a tiny bathroom and play up the gray tones of the marble countertop.**

CREATIVE CONTRAST

above, far right **Vanilla and turquoise hues repeat in a grouping of framed wallpaper samples, a statuesque lamp, and cushy seating. The espresso-stained console table inserts a bit of gravitas into the vignette.**

SHIPSHAPE QUARTERS

right **Navy makes a nautical splash as striped walls, patterned pillows, embellished linens, and denim coverlets. Running the wall stripes horizontally visually expands the small room.**

COASTAL ATTITUDE

right **Beachy browns, driftwood tans, and sail-crisp whites pop off deep-blue-sea walls that cozy up a sitting room.**

REVISITING RURAL

far right **Country blues take a pastel turn toward a summer cottage look to color-coordinate this farmhouse kitchen with a festive dishware collection.**

Q&A

Q: I love my blue-and-brown color scheme, but it needs an update. What colors will make good palette partners?

A: The way to update this classic pairing is to bring in bold leaf green, ivory, and citrus yellow for your throw pillows. Every room needs a bit of citrus pop.

ELAINE GRIFFIN
INTERIOR DESIGNER

straw
Honey tones set ceilings and walls aglow and pleasantly partner with brown, orange, and sage.

cream
Paint woodwork warm white to keep bright yellow walls looking cheerful; bright whites tend to make yellows go gray.

egg yolk
This sun-kissed tone complements dark colors and vivid hues and heats up looks from Old World to contemporary.

banana
Pair this muted yellow with sage greens, rich russets, and grayish blues to fashion naturally serene quarters.

butter
Buttery neutrals perform nicely on expansive walls and kitchen cabinets, and as counterweights to taxicab yellow.

yellow

No matter the intensity, yellow always packs a cheery punch, sparks interest, and convivially complements most every other color.

sunshine
An energetic hue, upbeat sunshine yellow spreads happiness and promotes optimism.

buttercream
Thanks to its sunrise/sunset undertones, this hue emits warmth and amplifies coziness.

vanilla
This handsome whispery yellow makes rooms feel expansive, calming, and graceful.

gold
Deeply toned yellows make civilized statements, appear luxurious, and enhance elegant interiors.

honey
Buzzing with feel-good vibrations, orange-yellows lift spirits and restore confidence.

lemon
Depending on its intensity, lemon can soften and soothe or add a zesty zing.

Color strategies. VISIBLE SHIFT.

The most visible of all colors, yellow boasts chameleonlike character, shifting its appearance with its surroundings. These noteworthy qualities make decorating with yellow challenging. CONSIDER QUANTITIES. Present lots of welcoming red-tinted yellows; use them on foyer and kitchen walls and as upholstery and drapery fabrics. Introduce cooler and more disruptive blue-tone yellows in smaller doses as accessories. THINK LIGHTER. Because yellow paint intensifies as it dries, pick a yellow you love, then buy a paint that's two or three shades lighter. EDIT WISELY. When using vivid yellow, add it one furniture piece or accessory at a time to ensure that your room doesn't resonate too loudly with techno-yellow vibes.

spunky yellow

"Humans are inevitably attracted to sunshine. In every society, yellow is a come-hither color."

—**Leatrice Eiseman,** color expert and consultant

Q&A

Q: I love yellow, but I'm afraid painting all the walls yellow in my room will be too intense. Any suggestions?

A: Ask the paint store to make a 50/50 mix of your chosen yellow and white. Paint the full strength color on the wall opposite the room's entry so it draws you in. Then use the lighter mix on the rest of the walls.

MARLAINA TEICH
INTERIOR DESIGNER

SHADES OF DIFFERENCE
above left **Vary intensity to create interest without ruffling a room's composure.** Honey-hue walls provide a peaceable backdrop for more saturated sunflower shades that materialize as patterned pillow shams, a textural coverlet, and nightstand accessories.

WARM WRAP
above **Choose red-flushed yellows to fashion convivial chambers.** In this dining room, a low-contrast combination of ocher walls and golden drapes luminously complements similarly colored furnishings and flooring while allowing an abstract canvas and sleek pendants to shine.

PROVIDE BALANCE
opposite **Vivid yellows can work on walls if you practice restraint when choosing furnishings.** Lush lemon walls give this living room a spritely lift that's beautifully counterbalanced by warm-white woodwork, buttercream furnishings, and taupe accessories.

Style setters

Strategically use yellows to expand your palette.

Swedish style. Combine buttery yellows and rich creams with Wedgwood blues to create cottage-comforting interiors. Include a lively mix of geometric fabrics to generate modern vibes.

Chic sophisticate. Be dramatic. Showcase formal furnishings upholstered in aubergine velvet and gold-striped purple draperies against tawny walls to shape high-fashion spaces.

Transitional designs. Fabricate laid-back schemes that easily accommodate your eclectic tastes. Paint walls taupe and move in sunshine-yellow, honey-gold, and teal furnishings.

Zesty spaces. Blend spice-trade shades, including saffron yellows, cinnamon oranges, and paprika reds, to create welcoming entertaining spaces and extra-cozy kitchens.

maize
This corncob color aptly adds country flavor to kitchen cabinets and dining room wainscots.

"Stay really pale on the walls so the yellow gives the room more of an overall feeling than a statement."
—Sara Gilbane, interior designer

pear
Paint foyer and bedroom walls in this friendly pear tone; accentuate the warmth with muted red and russet accents.

electric yellow
Electric yellow pulsates, so pair it with dusty greens, muted blues, and grayish purples to keep its psychedelic vibes in check.

saffron
Distribute saffron as bright spots of color in neutral schemes or introduce it as streamlined furnishings in white-walled contemporary spaces.

mustard
Deep yellows make an impact when introduced via touchable textiles such as velvet, corduroy, cashmere, chenille, and pseudo suedes.

ASCENDING ORDER
above right **Golden tones on the rug, chair, pillow, and draperies draw attention up and around this room.**

APT ANCHORS
above, far right **Use navy and black accents and furnishings to ground high-flying yellow and orange-yellow tones.**

SYNCHRONIZED SHADES
right **The vanity cabinet and green towels both sport yellow undertones, which pick up on the wall color.**

COMPLEMENTARY PARTNERS
below right **Bright yellow draperies and deep purple walls take center stage in a neutrally furnished room.**

WAKE-UP CALL
far right **Sunrise-yellow walls cheerfully highlight creamy glazed cabinets, stainless-steel appliances, and a buttery-yellow island.**

Q&A

Q: Since light can affect my room's color, what should I be aware of when decorating with yellow?
A: Golden yellow can be tricky in the way it reacts to light. Fluorescent light tends to bring out the green in golds, while natural light makes shades more yellow. A combination of natural and artificial light is the best way to showcase gold in all its glory.

DAVID BROMSTAD
DESIGNER AND TV HOST

crimson
Indicating good fortune, crimson is a gotta-have-it hue for creating traditional and Asian-inspired spaces.

brick
Anchor high-ceilinged and light-colored rooms with brick red wainscots, kitchen cabinets and islands, and painted floors.

hot pink
Pair flashy red-hot pinks with spring greens and bright whites to fashion fresh and lively cottage schemes.

radish
Va-va-voom radish reds make a statement when used for accents and furnishings in neutral rooms.

begonia
Display vivid magentas as accessories or as painted interiors on bookcases, alcoves, and deep-set windows.

red

Create spaces that demand attention by introducing glimmers, flashes, or explosions of red—the warm shade that burns the hottest.

ruby
Always stimulating and lively, intoxicating reds accelerate heartbeats and boost energy.

grenadine
Falling fetchingly between coral and pink, these shades emit tropical be-happy vibes.

chili pepper
Intensely spicy and warm, chili red indicates confidence, passion, and contentment.

garnet
Brownish reds create soul-warming spaces that feel insulated, safe, and reassuring.

cabernet
Dark wine reds promote tranquillity, offer a warm welcome, and make large rooms cozy.

lipstick pink
Soothing love-connection color evokes romantic rhythms and generous feelings.

Color strategies. **FIRED UP.** A potent pick-me-up, red packs a physical and psychological punch. It stimulates appetites, quickens breathing, and raises blood pressure. This powerhouse can overwhelm a room and its occupants, so proceed cautiously. **ASSESS AMOUNTS AND APPLICATIONS.** Go bold by painting walls orange-red, but ease red's impact with neutral furnishings. Take the middle road, using rosy red as the dominant color. Or simply spark interest by adding a red chair or burgundy sofa. **COMPARISON SHOP.** Shiny red fabrics look more vibrant than red cottons or wools, so bring textiles home to see how they work together and with other reds in a room. **FUN HOUSE!** Add inexpensive red accents, such as teakettles, towels, throws, pillows, and posters, to brighten rooms.

energetic red

"Although large doses of red make a loud statement, many people find it soothing when it has a muted purple undercurrent."

—Erinn Valencich, interior designer

Q&A

Q: How can I use dark red on my walls and avoid a formal look?
A: Red is a classic because it's so versatile. With mahogany furniture, it goes very traditional. With streamlined pieces, it's 20th-century modern. I love red with midrange khakis, grays, or taupes to get a combination that Europeans have used for centuries.

ELAINE GRIFFIN
INTERIOR DESIGNER

KINDRED SPIRITS
above left Present brilliant reds in varying sheens to keep their boldness in check. Orangey reds from the woven drapery fabric repeat in the glossy tomato-hue table and deep orange-red stools—an arrangement counterbalanced by the island's deeper matte finish.

QUIET QUARTERS
above This red reading room feels relaxed, thanks to its neutral components. Brown upholstery highlights accessories, while the long, low sideboard and backless shelf let the wood wall shine, which eases the red's impact.

PEACEMAKING PARTNERS
opposite Cherry red walls make a loft livable and lively, but could easily appear strident if left undressed. Cool blues, seen here in the artwork, sofa, and pillow, turn down the volume, as do black frames and white and gray furnishings.

Style setters

Use reds to expand your palette and enrich your home's style.

Timeless scenes. Traditional interiors call for deep maroons, mahoganies, rubies, or burgundies, accented with pale yellows, porcelain blues, and antique rugs sporting red and gold highlights.

Jazzy rhythms. Rethink 1960s psychedelic patterns and palettes (bright red, fuchsia, tangerine, banana, sky blue, and leafy green) to fashion retro modern designs. Try Op Art-patterned accent pillows in day-glow reds, pinks, and oranges to wake up a neutral sofa.

Country classic. Build country interiors around barn reds. Their blackened tones go nearly neutral when combined with soft blues, pale rose, harvest gold, and sage green.

Transitional tones. Deeper shades fashion spaces that suit eclectic preferences. Set bronze-coral and russet furnishings in front of light gray walls; finish the look with black and slate blue accents.

> "Pink looks best in a room with abundant natural light. Then it can glow and step away from the neutrals."
> —**Lori Deeds Carlton,** interior designer

tea rose
Tea rose makes a statement without overdoing. It's a good choice for transitional spaces such as entries and hallways.

mimosa
Deep pink mimosa cultivates garden cheer. Display it as solid-hue slipcovers and bedspreads accented with flowery pillows.

russet
Create warmly welcoming entertaining spaces by painting family room, living room, and dining room walls in rich russet tones.

blush
A nostalgic "grandma's attic" hue, red-warmed blush pink is a convivial choice for powder rooms and guest quarters.

cameo
Cameo's bronze notes shine as accents in warm-red rooms, as glazed furniture and cabinet finishes, and as ceramic-tiled walls or floors.

STATEMENT PIECES
above right **A grouping of raspberry-red chairs draws attention to the center of a neutrally dressed room.**

POWER COUPLE
above, far right **Gleaming gold finishes perfectly partner with most any red, including those shades of coral.**

MAKING WAVES
right **Hot pink makes this dining room impossible to ignore. The undulating patterned rug and batik-print curtain panels add liveliness to the traditional furnishings.**

SOPHISTICATED STAGE
below right **Striking burgundy walls spotlight the chic colors, finishes, and silhouettes of classically elegant furnishings.**

PRETTY PATTERNS
below, far right **Fruity reds take a relaxing turn, appearing as strawberry in the chair fabric and a more vivid cranberry in the rug.**

Q&A

Q: I love pink, but I don't want to make our family spaces overtly feminine. Can I use it and avoid a girly look?

A: Men and women wear blush pinks as an alternative to creams and beiges. The same is now true in the home. A blush pink is a great neutral that can be used for carpet, on a wall, or on a big piece of solid upholstery.

BRANDI HAGEN
INTERIOR DESIGNER

clover
Use spring-has-sprung clover-hued accessories to revive winter-weary kitchens, mudrooms, and powder rooms.

spinach
Spinach fuels interest on feature walls and as furniture finishes; it's a mighty-fine foil for fuchsia and periwinkle accents.

aloe
Accentuate aloe walls with dark wood finishes to create spa-like baths and exercise spaces.

celadon
This pale neutral with whispery blue undertones warms walls while visually stretching small spaces.

peapod
Decrease stress by painting offices, dens, and media rooms in ever-peaceful peapod.

green

Leafing out in an array of verdant shades, this versatile hue naturally enhances most every scheme and establishes moods from soothing to scintillating.

grass
Bright green indicates prosperity, growth, and security, which in turn creates happy spaces.

citron
Sunny yellow undertones produce a fashionable color that energizes interiors and uplifts spirits.

ivy
This true-green shade quietly grounds a space while evoking feelings of stability.

turquoise
One of the coziest greens, this bluish hue denotes safety and shapes restful retreats.

moss
Recalling woodland walks, this forest-floor color nourishes and soothes the soul.

pistachio
Very easy to live with, blue-tinged pistachio boosts a room's comfort quotient.

Color strategies. MIXED SIGNALS.
Greens can be active, passive, or a bit of both, generating high drama, fashioning playful places, and creating neutral backdrops. **NOTE TEMPERATURES.** Bluish greens, such as teal and turquoise, add cool luxury; warmer greens, such as olive and lime, emit contemporary vibes; midtone greens, including jade and fern, transition between warm and cool. **GO MONOCHROMATIC.** Layer light to dark shades of a single hue and accent the all-green scene with a vibrant accent color such as coral or eggplant. **CULTIVATE QUICK-CHANGE COLOR.** Introduce greens with solid or patterned pillows, rugs, slipcovers, and bed linens. Display topiaries and terrariums. Or simply fill glass containers with limes, green hydrangeas, or boxwood boughs.

dewy greens

> "In places where there isn't a lot of light, choose greens that have more white. Moody gray-greens hold up well in sunnier locations."
>
> —**Kishani Perera,** interior designer

Q&A

Q: How can I use an olive or avocado green without straying into 1970s decorating territory?

A: If you want a muted green, test paint samples. What seems like khaki on the chip could be vibrant olive on the wall. Keep potential accent colors, like peony pink, in mind to prevent the earthy greens from looking drab.

RUTHIE SOMMERS
INTERIOR DESIGNER

PLAYFUL PRESENTATION
above left **Color-swatch boards and a capricious canvas showcased on bottle-green walls make a "go big or go home" statement that repeats in the lively colorful patterned pillows piled on a jade green sofa.**

BALANCED BLEND
above **Pair bright apple greens with softer lemon-lime walls and brown accents to create serene sanctuaries. The solid-green bedstead makes an impact, while the striped bench presents the same green in a more understated way.**

PERIOD PERFECT
opposite **Look to your home's origins for color inspiration. This remodeled kitchen in an early-20th-century home seems suitably vintage thanks to Victorian green cabinets, charcoal-hue soapstone counters, and copper cookware.**

Style setters

Use greens to expand your palette and enhance your home's style.

Summery spaces. Create a citrusy splash in kitchens, sunrooms, and hobby spaces. Set lime green, zesty orange, and lemon yellow accessories against turquoise walls for a fresh take on tropical.

Rethink timeless. Update a traditional green-and-blue pairing. Showcase apple-green toile or floral chintz draperies against sky blue walls. Enhance the revitalized scheme with raspberry and pale pink accents.

Classic comforts. Formalize libraries and dining rooms with opulent hues. Paint walls hunter green, move in dark tables, moss green velvet chairs, navy fabrics, and gilded flourishes.

Spicy quarters. Set salsa red, burnt orange, maize, jalapeño green, and lime green furnishings and trimmings against guacamole-hue walls to create saucy spaces.

kiwi
Tie adjacent spaces together by painting walls a soft, but still kicky, kiwi green.

"Look outside to see what colors are paired with green. Usually those deep pinks, blues, browns, and whites will look great inside, too."
—**Stephanie Wohlner,** interior designer

olive
Apply olive tones to your walls via luminescent glazes that showcase the color's golden undertones.

avocado
Down but not out, avocado returns as make-a-statement walls, sofas, and draperies in modern interiors.

celery
Ever-crisp and clean, celery snaps to attention when paired with olive and ruby tones.

apple green
This fresh-faced green pops up everywhere because it nicely complements both strong and pastel hues.

TONAL PROGRESSIONS
above right **Turquoise** linens draw attention to a seafoam green bedstead, which directs the eye to a like-colored painting.

MASTERFUL MIX
above, far right **Chartreuse** on the draperies sets a dramatic stage for a chair upholstered in a breezy complementary stripe.

HIGH IMPACT
right **Shiny white** woodwork, cabinetry, and photo mats winningly contrast against kelly green walls.

BAND TOGETHER
below right **Enhance the** excitement by displaying your scheme's most vivid shades, such as this brilliant grass green, as solid blocks of color.

NATURAL COMPANIONS
below, far right **Wood** finishes, soapstone counters, and celery-color cabinets create a calm work space where creativity thrives.

Q&A

Q: **Lime green seems like a natural with other citrus hues, but what other color combos create a fresh palette?**

A: Paired with blue-greens, coral, and raspberry, citrus lime is striking. For a more subdued palette, paint café au lait-like browns on walls and use muted lime for furniture fabric and accents.

PHILLIPA RADON
COLOR EXPERT

shrimp
Use this nearly neutral shade to warm bathrooms, softly color bedroom walls, and visually lower high ceilings.

blood orange
This combustible color fires up living-area walls and sparks interest as furniture and cabinet finishes.

papaya
Promote a sense of arrival by displaying this tropical tone on entryway walls or as a focal-point wall in a living area.

coral
Highlight this always-hip hue with bright-white woodwork and ceilings painted a lighter coral.

tangerine
This citrusy orange works well as accessories to brighten rooms with chocolate brown or lime green walls.

orange

Whether it's apricot, amber, peach, terra-cotta, or tangerine, oranges supply house-warming options that support styles ranging from Old World to psychedelic.

pumpkin
This saturated shade warms the soul by evoking images of fiery autumn foliage and fall harvests.

terra-cotta
Whether on walls or as saltillo-tile floors, this burnished tone transports spirits to Mediterranean climes.

peach
Delicate in nature, pale peach creates romantic rooms with feminine flair.

ginger
Brown-tinted orange takes on spicy overtones that heat up spaces and suggest an exotic or global style.

brick
Like the material it simulates, this reddish-brown hue represents strength and endurance.

salmon
Combining red-orange and yellow-orange creates a sense of harmonious abundance.

Color strategies. **CONSIDER ORANGE.**
The warm hue downsizes too-large rooms, stimulates appetites and conversations, and draws folks into a space. **DO A TEST RUN.** Because paint colors deepen as they dry and darken with each successive coat, brush swaths in varying shades on different walls before making your selection. Since you will probably need two coats for your finished product, apply a second layer to each shade. Note how the swatches look day and night. **NOT SOLD ON TRUE ORANGE?** Set walls and ceiling glowing with softer shades such as pale peach or orange-flushed tans. **PROPER PARTNERS.** Oranges play nicely with navy blue, turquoise, yellow, red, hot pink, lime, and forest green. **MAKE A SPLASH.** Introduce the cheery hue in table linens, casual dishware, and patterned pillows.

juicy orange

"If you're thinking of painting a room red, consider a melon instead. Both are saturated colors, but melon is more elegant, unexpected, and sophisticated."

—**Katie Ridder,** *interior designer*

Q&A

Q: How do I keep a room with orange walls from feeling too warm?
A: Include a splash of turquoise. It's like adding water to fire. Or pair it with dark chocolate for a sophisticated look or with soft yellow for a young, cheery look.

KELLY BERG
COLOR CONSULTANT

ADD DIMENSION
above left **Introduce true orange in a dining room to encourage lively dialogue, but soften its impact with a paint treatment that blends in lighter orange and gold glazes. Emphasize the glowing walls with white woodwork and neutral furnishings.**

APT ACCENTS
above **Oranges set against yellow backdrops wake up breakfast rooms. Incorporate oranges, ranging from deep russet to light peach, in seat cushions and pillows. Include patterned shades for light fixtures and flowery pillows that feature all the room's colors.**

GO MOD
opposite **Tangerine walls work with natural woodwork, a light-finish table, and curvaceous chairs to give an eating area a contemporary kick. Red-tinted oranges on artwork, dishware, and floorboards stress an orange-rules design philosophy.**

Style setter

Use varying orange shades to expand your palette and enhance your home's style.

Classic applications. Like traditional? Opt for understated shades such as copper, brick, or burnt orange. Grapey purples, turquoise, and sage make unexpectedly elegant partners for these orangey jewel tones.

Global influences. Got a yen for the exotic? Start with spicy ginger, cinnamon, or cayenne and blend in bright pinks, reds, turquoise, and tawny gold to create well-traveled tableaus.

Modern medleys. Crave cutting edge? Combine zesty oranges with equally vivid tones of periwinkle blue, lime green, and yellow to create spaces that pulsate with fashion-forward vibes.

Tranquil transition. Longing for peace and quiet? Paint walls in honey-orange hues, and layer in caramel-shade furnishings and saturated coral and muted aquamarine accents.

seashell
Fluctuating between pink and orange, this seashell-like shade dazzles in rooms filled with natural light.

tea rose
This perennially charming color makes a comeback in guest rooms or girly-girl boudoirs and baths.

persimmon
Present this red-tinted color on spirit-warming walls, kicky slipcovers, or zesty accents.

flamingo
Accessories in this pretty midtone complement all the other shades showcased here.

bittersweet
Use this flamboyant shade to establish styles ranging from retro kitsch to Palm Beach chic.

"When you have a really small room where there's no way you're going to make it look big, make it dramatic with a dark rusty hue."
—**Cecilie Starin,** interior designer

FIRED UP
above right **Black, stainless-steel, and white surfaces accentuate flashy persimmon-hue cabinets that warm up this contemporary space.**

PEACEFUL PALETTE
above, far right **Shades of apricot, peach, and coral and complementary patterned fabrics fashion a serene scene.**

OPPOSITES ATTRACT
right **Complementary colors appear more vibrant when placed next to each other, as this pumpkin wall and blue-striped rug prove.**

COLOR BLAST
below right **Neutral upholstery fabrics and breezy white curtains allow this vibrant coral-dominated palette to shine.**

TWO-PART HARMONY
far right **Integrate oranges from both sides of the yellow-to-red spectrum to create captivatingly high-contrast compositions. When splashing on a vivid hue, figure your paint needs carefully to ensure the saturated color covers well. To calculate the quantity you need, go to** *BHG.com/howmuchpaint.*

Q&A

Q: I love orange, but I'm afraid the fruity color will be too overwhelming on my walls. What shade would work best as a room color?
A: Much of orange's shock value goes away when you pick a shade with some brownness. I tend to choose bold colors, but I also always like them with a little "mud" in them.

JACKIE TERRELL
INTERIOR DESIGNER

fuchsia
Muted magenta
warms walls, lowers
ceilings, and kicks
up its heels as flirty
skirted slipcovers.

orchid
Use this whispery
mauve to lighten
woodwork, upper
walls, or ceilings in
mainly mauve spaces.

hibiscus
A must-have accent
for garden themes, it
partners beautifully
with grassy greens
and periwinkles.

magenta
Paint bookcase
interiors a vibrant
fuchsia or combine
the hot hue with red
for a progressive
punch.

mauve
Set this refreshed
shade against coffee-
hue walls or pair it
with apricots and
apple greens.

purple

Combining cool blues and warm reds, the purple palette supplies a striking array of color options for decorating traditional and unconventional interiors.

violet
Bring a sense of security while encouraging creative thinking with this convivial hue.

berry
Here's a lively purple hue that energizes and adds a touch of mystery.

wisteria
This palest of blue-tone purples promotes peaceful, easy feelings.

lavender
An old-fashioned favorite, lavender excites and reassures at the same time.

grape
Deep purple hints at untold riches, evokes passion, and feels luxurious.

periwinkle
With bright-blue undertones, this cheerful shade always sounds a feel-good note.

Color strategies. **PURPLE PURSUITS.**

Purple veers from majestic and passionate in its deeper tones to sweet and innocent as a newborn baby in its palest incarnations. Purple's fluctuating tones can make it a challenging color to weave into our homes. **PRIVATE VERSUS PUBLIC.** Generally, dark purples such as aubergine work best in formal living and dining areas; bright purples energize kids' and craft rooms; lavender fashions soothing backgrounds in bedrooms and baths. **MASTER THE MIX.** Combine pink- and blue-tinted purples, such as magenta, violet, and lilac, in varying intensities to create pleasing compositions. **GO NEUTRAL.** Though browns and whites make fine companions, pearl to battleship grays and shimmering silver give purple schemes updated appeal.

purple passion

> "Plum is a surprisingly versatile color. It's super fresh with greens, from lime to oregano. I also love it with turquoise, gold, and orange."
>
> —Elaine Griffin, interior designer

Q&A

Q: Since purple comes from both the warm and cold sides of the color wheel, how do I choose pairings?

A: For a glamorous look, pair purples with gray. For a more feminine approach, partner it with white. Brown tones warm and enrich a purple palette.

JEFFREY BILHUBER
INTERIOR DESIGNER

LUXURIOUS LAIR
above left Lushly layered purples draw the eye through this elegantly appointed boudoir. Lavender walls frame a niche covered in eggplant-hue wallpaper; berry tones swirl on the area rug; and shimmery and woven royal purple fabrics dress the bed and windows. Rich wood tones add warmth, while mirrored surfaces create sparkle and light.

FORMAL ATTIRE
above Grape-painted walls and woodwork combine with deep gold tones to modernize a design without hampering its sophisticated spirit. The walls highlight lighter-hue furnishings, golden finishes, and boldly patterned draperies that feature the room's two complementary hues.

LADYLIKE RETREAT
opposite Pink-tinted and blue-tone purples combine to fashion fetchingly feminine accommodations. Though bright fuchsia and dusty grape pop on the window and bedstead and perky pillows dress the bed, the soothing lilac walls and lavender coverlet encourage romantic reveries.

Style setter

Use varying shades of purple to expand your palette and enhance your home's style.

Elegant outlook.
Accent deep-purple walls with neutral upholstered pieces; metallic patinas; plush textiles; dark finishes; and gold, caramel, and/or burnt orange accents to strike a sophisticated chord.

Cottage charm.
Combine garden patterns and colors, including blue-shaded violet and hyacinth, hot pink, marigold yellow, and leaf green, to create vintage character.

Eclectic allure.
Paint walls deep mauve and bring in sage green furniture, spicy orange and harvest gold fabrics, and dusty amethyst and gray accessories.

Fashionably funky.
Use deep lavender walls to highlight fuchsia, lime green, cobalt blue, turquoise, and tomato-red accessories and coordinating big-motif fabrics.

"If you want a lavender room that's not girly, add elements such as black-and-white photography, industrial pieces, and streamlined furniture."

—**Kelly Berg,** interior designer

hyacinth
This pleasing hue works equally well with deep purples, other lavenders, and its farther-removed magenta cousins.

iris
Combine blue iris with hyacinth and lilac accents to create calmly monochromatic bedrooms.

lilac
Lilac cools down too-sunny spaces, visually expands tiny rooms, and highlights all purple shades.

amethyst
Pale jewel tones contribute graceful rhythms to girly-girl bedrooms and bathrooms.

violet
Use this spring-fresh hue to brighten walls, revive tired furnishings, and animate yellow rooms.

BRIGHT LIGHTS
above right **Mulberry paint lowers a ceiling, while grayish lavender cabinets give the room a contemporary lift.**

NEUTRAL TOUCH
above, far right **Lavender's girly side is tempered by beige upholstery and window fabrics, black accents, and iron furnishings.**

USE COMPLEMENTS
right **Lavender agreeably allies with lemony yellows, its color-wheel complement, and rich browns in this slightly sassy bedroom.**

UNEXPECTED PARTNERS
below right **Cool blues, vibrant yellows, and hot oranges unite with more-formal furnishings for collected charm.**

CREATIVE CONTRAST
below, far right **Fashionable white and green furnishings update a room decorated in violet, lavender, and lilac shades.**

Q&A

Q: I've been told purple is a challenging color to decorate with. How can I be sure to get it right?

A: If purple makes you color shy, test the waters by adding hits of hyacinth—as an accent wall, an accessory, or one standout pillow—to a room full of subtle, neutral patterns and textures.

SARA STORY
INTERIOR DESIGNER

camel
Use a spicy brown to create a dramatic focal-point wall or to heat up rooms on the north side of your home.

khaki
Incorporate tan walls and khaki upholstery fabrics as backdrops that spotlight a diverse array of colors and patterns.

putty
Alternatives to bright white, putty-color paints give a contemporary lift to woodwork, ceilings, hallway walls, and built-in cabinetry.

sand
Combining this seashore tone with azure blues, aquamarines, and sunny yellows will fashion cottage-style digs.

neutrals

Neutral hues emphasize vibrant colored and patterned companions, unify contrasting palettes, and establish styles ranging from peaceable to progressive.

beige
This brownish shade with masculine undertones evokes relaxing and reassuring rhythms.

gray
The colors of granite and concrete, grays and silvers create rock-solid looks with enduring style.

cream
Buttery whites boast a lush depth that warms too-cool spaces and encourages calm.

brown
This convivial color denotes reliability and stability that promotes cocooning.

heather
Soothingly saturated shades in gray tones spark plenty of interest without overpowering.

taupe
The grayish-brown tone is favored for its go-with-anything nature and laid-back vibes.

Color strategies. **ACTING RANGE.**
Warm neutrals, such as brown, tan, ivory, gold, and black, and cool neutrals, including white, silver, lavender, and gray, effortlessly move between supporting and starring roles in a room. **CHECK THEIR TRUE COLORS.** Many neutrals sport undertones from blue to yellow to red, which need to be considered when devising a palette. **TONE ON TONE.** Employ varying shades of one color to create layers of interest. More closely related shades, such as vanilla, cream, and pale yellow, fashion serene schemes that shift with the changing light. **STRENGTHEN ASSOCIATIONS.** Carry the same neutrals from room to room—via painted trim, patterned fabrics, and furniture finishes—to forge cohesive connections.

no-fail neutrals

"Because we live in such a color-filled, busy world, coming home to a calm, neutral space feels like a breath of fresh air."

—**Kelly Keiser,** interior designer

Q&A

Q: I own a dark brown sofa. How can I keep the piece from dominating the look of the room?

A: I love brown sofas. You can put any color pillow on it. Keep the walls lighter, anchor the space with a light textural rug, and limit other dark browns to an accent chair or a picture frame. Bring in midtones such as hot pink, red, and teal.

NADIA GELLER
INTERIOR DESIGNER

PUNCTUATION POINTS

above left **Yellow** and white accessories explode onto the monochromatic scene. Midtone bluish grays in the patterned pillow and ottoman balance the room's brighter accessories, the gray fireplace and sofa, and the black details on the firebox and furniture.

TEXTURAL ARRAY

above **Shiny light fixtures, woven baskets, a distressed desk,** and stony flooring spread textural interest throughout this office area. To perk up the neutral vibe, shots of blue and turquoise play off the pale blue walls.

MOTIF MAGIC

opposite **When** introducing patterns, consider size and contrast. This low-contrast area rug provides an appealing anchor for chairs sporting smaller-patterned seats. The table base, pendant shade, and wood sculptures contribute shapely silhouettes that add to the medley of motifs.

Style setter

Use a range of neutrals to expand your palette and enhance your home's style.

Rethink the classics. Combine silver, charcoal gray, and white with misty mauve for understated elegance, or rev up that combo with navy blue and pale yellow accents.

Urbane attitude. Modern, manly digs call for streamlined palettes. Paint walls deep brown, add caramel leather and beige linen upholstered pieces, and introduce one vibrant hue via pillows and artwork.

Green scenes. Take a cue from Mother Nature. Combine light herbal greens and natural wood finishes with gold, lavender, and black accessories to create quietly chic spaces.

Industrial cool. Set stainless-steel surfaces, white lacquered furniture, and black-and-white photographs against textured charcoal walls; moor the look with a graphic area rug.

lilac
Choose neutrals with a bluish or purple cast to introduce another layer of color into mostly neutral rooms.

"If you're the kind of person who agonizes between six blue-grays, use a natural material you love, like tile or stone, to help you make the selection."
—Rebekah Zaveloff, *kitchen designer*

light gray
Peace-promoting pale grays work wonderfully with other grays, deep lavenders, pastel pinks, and pale greens.

pale blue
Spotlight this pale blue shade with white woodwork, tan accessories, and pickled furniture finishes.

alabaster
Unlike bright white, alabaster warms woodwork, visually lowers ceilings, and lessens the contrast when combined with vibrant tones.

sprout
Blend barely-there green with dark wood finishes, clear-glass accessories, and stony surfaces to advance peace and harmony.

25¢ le chic
GUARANTEED WASHABLE

NEUTRAL GROUND
above right A rug's colors repeat in darker and bolder patterned pillows that pop atop beige furniture.

NOTEWORTHY PATTERN
above, far right Chairs matching the wall color still explode into view thanks to the fabric's off-white trellis motif.

ARTFULLY ACCESSORIZED
right Add glamour to a small bath with silver and gray. Tile and coutertop provide the deep gray background while silver brings in the bling. Hammered metal pieces and woven baskets add warming texture.

SIMPLY SPECTACULAR
below right Pearl-gray walls accentuate bright-white, plush lavender, and gray-tone textiles and gilded finishes.

TONAL SHIFTS
far right The flooring's khaki and stone hues repeat in varying intensities to unify living, dining, and cooking areas.

Q&A

Q: How do I keep a gray room from looking too cold and uninviting?
A: The right materials will keep gray from being cold. In a gray room, add patinated furniture, natural rugs like sisal, lots of linen, and warm wood tones.

JONATHAN RACHMAN
INTERIOR DESIGNER

using color in rooms

Discover palette ideas for every room in your home, and learn how to layer shades and textures for a look that's uniquely you.

BOLD BEGINNINGS
Transition spaces such as entryways, hallways, and staircases are ideal places to go all out with vivid hues.

entries

Make sure guests know they've truly arrived by creating lively entryways that issue a warm welcome while previewing stylish pleasures to come.

Color strategies. SPACE-RELATED CHALLENGES.

Though they tend to be small, front foyers and back-door entryways pose design dilemmas aplenty. These come-on-in spaces, which connect to the outdoors and to other rooms, play important roles in how your home looks, feels, and functions. You can turn an entryway into a hospitable hub that harmonizes with the whole through strategic placement of color and pattern. **ASSESS ACCESS.** Look into the entryway from outside. Note visible walls and architectural elements in adjoining spaces to take in connections that will need addressing. **FRIENDLY GREETING.** No hues say "Stay awhile" better than warm tones; cozy up entries by introducing reds, yellows, and oranges on walls, fabrics, and area rugs. **CREATE EFFORTLESS TRANSITIONS.** Pull a color palette from a multihue area rug, painting, drapery fabric, or upholstered piece to introduce in the entry and personalize with complementary accents. Draw from this scheme as you decorate adjacent spaces, shifting wall colors to maximize impact. **ESTABLISH STYLE AND TONE.** Entryways—whether grand or diminutive—provide a place for announcing your preference for formal or casual interiors. Consider how you can use wallpaper designs, fabric patterns, and color schemes—from jewel tones to neon chromes to vintage combos—to relay refined charm, contemporary spirit, or informal appeal.

try this combo

Pick three or four colors to carry from front door to back. Mix in a high-energy hue such as yellow; noteworthy neutrals; and plush, gauzy, and rough textures to build interest.

touch of metal
A bit of metallic shimmer adds glamour to furnishings and artwork.

make connections
In adjacent rooms, natural blinds echo the feel of the entry bench.

warm things up
Textural fabrics such as this embroidered velvet add warmth to a sparsely furnished entry space.

get cozy
A thick, nubby throw can inject a quick pop of portable color that can move from room to room as needed.

visual subtlety
When colors are this vibrant, it's a good idea to create a subtle pattern play. The tone-on-tone striped wall quietly asserts itself.

firm footing
Elegant walnut hardwood flooring creates a visual flow from the entry to other rooms.

provide a link
A lively rug in cool tones makes the connection between the purple dining room and golden foyer and living room.

on the wall
Even a narrow wall can accommodate a vertically stacked trio of brilliant color prints.

COLORFUL GREETING
The tone-on-tone striped walls give visitors a glimpse of the rich color used throughout this vibrantly hued home.

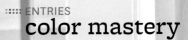

color mastery

Link prettily furnished foyers to living spaces with color-coordinated displays of brightly hued knickknacks, statuesque lamps, and garden-fresh forms.

MAGNIFY APPEAL
Hang mirrors to reflect colorful pieces in adjacent spaces and make entryways feel bigger.

Paint storage and seating elements to further your color and decorating theme.

GET READY!
above right Flashy fabric bins and carryalls can repeat accent colors from elsewhere in the home.

ENHANCE VIEWS
above, far right Liven up a mostly-white entry or mudroom with kids' artwork, plush pillows, and striped cushions.

DUO TONES
middle right Install white wainscot or chair rails on richly painted walls to add contrast and convey sophisticated substance in formal foyers.

WALL INSPIRATION
middle, far right The warm russets of a brick wall suggested the color palette for this inviting entry. Red repeats in the painted dresser, rug, and houndstooth pillow.

OPT FOR POP
right Light-color wood elements paired with strong wall and accent colors prevent an entry from making a bland first impression.

TRY TRENDS
far right A bold painted dresser personalizes the entry palette, but can be updated when you want to try a new trendy hue.

pattern mastery

Select marvelous motifs, picture-perfect prints, tantalizing textiles, and furniture with striking silhouettes to create remarkable reception areas.

THINK RETRO

above **Collected dishware with diminutive designs hangs as artwork and complements the large-scale vintage patterns for pillows on the old garden seat. The seat's complex pattern is set off by the French-blue beaded board wainscoting.**

TRY PLAYFUL

above right **An area rug with an animated pattern makes a sassy statement against the subtly striped walls. The wall's leafy motif and the brown-embellished pillow play off the rug's hues and flowerlike pattern, which add another layer of interest.**

NATURE'S BOUNTY

opposite left **When plying patterns in nature-inspired settings, remember that stone and metal surfaces, woven baskets, and wood floors contribute a pattern of textures. Allow earthen elements to shine by piling in understated geometric fabrics in forest and field tones.**

GEOMETRY CLASS

opposite right **Classically styled trellis wallpaper references the great outdoors. Set off by white painted woodwork, the wallpaper pattern also plays off the door's geometric lattice details.**

Cue the out-of-doors

Ease the transition between indoors and out by introducing perennially charming alfresco colors, sisal rugs, botanical images, and earthen surfaces. Plant an idea. Like other harvested-from-nature materials, plants contribute pattern-making forms. Stress the in-and-out connection by arranging architectural branches in a tall green glass vase. Bring in towering topiaries, perk up a table with potted succulents, display floral arrangements, or set out a single potted ficus tree to visually signal that an environmental change is under way. Add garden decor. Outdoor decorative elements look charming in an entry. Use an outdoor planter as an umbrella stand or employ a rustic potting bench as an entry table. Frame vintage seed packets in matching black frames to hang on the wall. Invite the critters inside with a frog or bird sculpture.

PEACEFUL HARMONY
Green walls highlight
tawny and copper shades.
Persimmon accents and
pillows tie the look to the
carpet and the artwork.

living rooms

Take your decorating cues from spaces designed and colorfully furnished in ways that promote congregating, conversing, and kicking back.

Color strategies.

LIVING LARGE. Even in small homes, living rooms, dens, and family rooms have to live large. They host a variety of activities—entertaining, playing games, watching TV, quiet reading. Usage may dictate how the space is laid out, but every living room benefits from a color palette that reflects its myriad functions. **MOODY HUES.** Painting walls in soothing shades of blue, green, or purple sets a serene stage. Warm reds and oranges invigorate, while yellows and neutrals play well with an array of accent colors, which expands your decorating options. **SEEK INSPIRATION.** Find color clues in a favorite artwork, fabric, or area rug, or in hues and patterns showcased elsewhere in your home. **FOCAL FEATURE.** Direct attention to a fireplace, panoramic vista, or media cabinet using a hue that stands out. Line a mantel with flamboyant accessories; frame views with colorful curtains; and tuck televisions into cabinets painted to contrast with the wall color. **CREATURE COMFORTS.** If you like to change things up with chromatic throws and pillows, opt for comfortable chairs and sofas covered in neutral-tone fabrics. Center conversation and media seating on an eye-catching patterned rug, and move in painted tables and storage pieces to hold drinks, books, and hobby materials. **ADD COLOR WHERE YOU CAN.** To keep things lively, use accessories to carry contrasting tones from corner to corner.

try this combo

Fashion calmingly convivial quarters with green and blue hues brightened by yellow.

set the scale
The largest and most vivid pattern guides the choice of pattern motif and scale for coordinating fabrics.

weighty matters
Olive-green accents, such as the faux-leather woven basket and the painted armoire, help ground the room.

simple scheme
An analogous palette of blues and greens with a jolt of warm yellow from the fabrics is an easy scheme to put together and to live with.

warm touch
Tactile neutral furnishings add warmth to the cool blues and greens. The multihue blend is a great choice for an active family space.

keep it natural
Woven blinds and baskets bring in more natural textures that balance the soft, puffy area rug.

Color clue
Use a bold hue from a main fabric pattern for a runner, pillows, and other accents.

FRESH FINISH
Furnishings, baskets, and
accessories in a variety of
painted, stained, and
natural shades add
another layer of interest.

color mastery

Spread color and pattern creatively to devise relaxing rooms that showcase your personality.

WAVES OF COLOR
Vibrant pillows catch the eye and echo a rainbow wall of brightly bound books grouped by color for visual effect.

Walls offer a large canvas, but accents bring color into your room.

BRIGHT CONTRAST
above right **Turquoise, pink, and gold partner to craft captivating quarters.**

ADD A STANDOUT
above, far right **Include one vividly patterned upholstered piece that complements your color scheme.**

SPICE IT UP
middle right **Orange throw pillows and lamps make an energetic splash in this icy-blue room.**

LAY GROUNDWORK
middle, far right **A carpet's brown and pumpkin colors repeat in varying tones on the sofa, cushions, pillows, and accessories.**

STAIRSTEP COLOR
right **Aligning orange, the strongest accent color, at ascending levels draws the eye into the room.**

BE ARTISTIC
far right **Paint a vintage table in a color pulled from a patterned fabric or from your color palette.**

color mastery | large spaces

Employ a few fool-the-eye tricks to make large rooms feel cozier without losing an inch of hanging-out space.

DIVIDE AND CONQUER

left These seating areas are linked with color, but each has its own identity. Beige chairs bracket the fireplace; a gold sofa defines the border of another conversation area; and blue acts as the tie that binds.

LOWER THE ROOF

above left Minimize wide-open spaces by conjuring up a false-ceiling illusion. Dark-hue blinds work in concert with ceiling beams to deceptively lower upper perimeters, which keeps attention focused within the colorfully accessorized ground-level conversation area.

MODIFY PARAMETERS

above Warm colors, including yellow, orange, and red, advance to visually condense too-large rooms (see "Reshape with color," opposite). In this living space, rust-color paint, which ties the ceiling to the draperies, makes the ceiling appear lower, while gold-hue walls create a cozier intimate feel by pulling the eye inward.

STRETCH BOUNDARIES
Define a central seating area with a colorful rug. Use brightly colored draperies and upholstery fabrics to direct attention to outlying seating.

Yellow Chiffon

Insect Wing

Pratt & Lambert
Paradise Lost

Reshape with color

Color affects how we perceive a room's size and influences how we feel when we're in the space. Strategically selected and placed colors visually stretch Lilliputian living rooms or shrink too-grand great rooms. When choosing paint colors, remember: Hot and cold. Cool blues, greens, and purples recede to open closed-in rooms and also cool sun-drenched spaces. Warm reds, yellows, and oranges move surfaces forward, causing big rooms to appear smaller and feel cozier. Expand and contract. Light hues on walls and ceiling increase the sense of space; dark hues do the opposite. Painting a long room's narrow walls a deep warm hue condenses the expanse. Alternatively, painting a room's walls to match adjoining spaces blurs borders and makes the smaller space appear larger.

color mastery | small spaces

Bring high-fashion style to diminutive rooms by using color-savvy tactics, editing tricks, and space-stretching strategies.

MINIMIZE MOTIFS

left Because patterns have more visual weight than unadorned surfaces, they can make small rooms appear smaller. Grow the perception of space by dressing plainly upholstered sofas with simply patterned pillows mixed with shapely cushions covered in textural solid fabrics.

INGENIOUS IDEA

above left When you're short on walls to color with paint, grab space from extra windows or unused doorways. Botanical paintings hung over the windows create a transition between indoors and out while mirroring the cool tones of the sunroom's fabrics and greenery.

SNUG FIT

above Got a penchant for cozy? Decorate with saturated tones that have a similar intensity and weight. In this taupe-walled haven, each stretch of color is balanced by a naturally neutral or light-hue accessory.

OPEN TO COLOR
left Opt for neutral walls, woven rugs, and white slipcovers to increase opportunities for exhibiting cottage-charming vintage accents and collections. Put open-weave pieces—such as lobster traps, fencing remnants, and old crates—on display to buoy interest without weighing down walls.

pattern mastery

Incorporate a handpicked selection of patterns and motifs to establish a theme, set a mood, and show your style.

LIVE EASY
This happy-hue palette of primary colors drawn from a natty striped fabric emits summery, laid-back vibes.

CARRIED AWAY
above right **Pops of blue carry the checked curtains' dominant shade into the seating area.**

PICTURE THIS
above, far right **Carry a graphic image throughout a space by selecting colorful fabrics that sport similar motifs.**

SHADE SHIFT
middle right **Blend low- and high-contrast patterns in vibrant and muted hues to amplify visual appeal.**

ARTISTIC ASSEMBLY
middle, far right **Mismatched furniture enhances a conversation grouping that is grounded by a complementary rug.**

WELL MATCHED
right **Designs appearing on the wall, rug, and draperies partner nicely because each pattern varies in size and echoes green touches.**

GO WIDE
far right **This narrow room is broadened visually by horizontally stacking two vibrant swaths of color and pattern.**

before & after

A pumped-up palette, style-forward fabrics, and color-coordinated furnishings make a once boring, inhospitable space a lively living room where folks love to gather.

3 color flaws

1 Spartan furnishings don't relate.

2 Walls and shaded windows lack pizzazz.

3 Color and pattern deficiencies make the room feel cold.

3 color fixes

1 Rearranged furniture makes room for a colorful chair and ottoman.

2 Artwork, accents, and banded curtains brighten perimeters.

3 Cheerful blocks of color create convivial rhythms.

Orange Appeal

Cinco de Mayo

Varsity Blues

Benjamin Moore
Barely Beige

Candy Green

Dramatic flair

Garner compliments galore by using brilliant blocks of color to energize bland, tired spaces.

Be intense. Choose saturated colors that boast a contemporary attitude. Spotlight the chromatic qualities of fabrics and accents with neutral walls and upholstery fabrics.

Rearrange furniture. Determine ways to lay out conversation areas that allow you to add extra seating or ottomans done up in colorful fabrics.

Update windows. Think of windows as additional opportunities for furthering the room's color story. Dress them in textural shades and brightly banded draperies.

Define the space. Choose a neutral textured area rug that's large enough to comfortably accommodate all the furniture pieces in each seating area.

Accent thoughtfully. Opt for curvaceous lamps, stack vibrant artwork, and display dishes that introduce quieter hues and rounded shapes.

STREAMLINE VIEWS
Bright pillows wearing understated motifs emphasize the dynamic color palette without visually cluttering the composition with busy patterns.

LONG-TERM CHOICES
Investing in timeless pieces ensures enduring style. Choose neutral colors, finishes, and fabrics for expensive, permanent, or difficult-to-change furnishings and flooring.

dining rooms

A color-filled palette and patterns in an array of textures create comfortable feast-for-the-eye dining rooms that encourage folks to linger.

Color strategies. **MAKE IT WORK.** Dining rooms, often pass-through zones between formal living areas and utilitarian kitchens, demand special attention. To ensure these areas garner the usage they deserve, decorate the space so it works with its neighbors and with your family's living and entertaining requirements. One of the easiest ways to forge connections and create stylish comfort is through color. **CONVIVIAL TINT.** Dressing windows with sunny yellow draperies, white-painted shutters, or breezy sheers keeps a room bright for daytime. Paint walls amber, peach, coral, red, or orange to create cocoonlike warmth that sparks after-dinner conversation. **DOUBLE DUTY.** Tuck in a comfy striped chair, a painted computer armoire, or a banquette that stows crafting supplies to expand your room's purpose. **MELD SPACES.** Carry similar colors and patterns into adjacent spaces; consider using varying tones of the same hue to give each room an individual point of view. **QUICK-CHANGE ACCESSORIES.** Brighten tables and sideboards with vibrant table runners, scintillating centerpieces, and displays of chromatic collections that play off fabrics in the dining room and adjoining areas. **SHIMMER AND SHINE.** Gleaming silver services, prismatic crystal chandeliers, and mirrored surfaces amplify natural and ambient light and magnify the impact of colorful accents. Together they visually enlarge the space.

try this combo

Opt for a nearly monochromatic yellow scheme. Marry maize to beige or cream neutrals and wood finishes with golden tones. Bright orange accents add zing.

orange pop
Small touches of orange on the dining table inject drama and interest without distorting the color palette.

playful pattern
In a room used mostly for early and midday meals, a cheery and energetic sunburst pattern is a playful choice for shades, cushions, and pillows.

sunny disposition
Maize yellow paint on the dining chairs ushers the sunny color into the middle of the room.

neutral backdrop
White walls, wainscot, and pillows let the soft shades of yellow shine without being bold. The wainscot pattern and the fabric texture make the white surfaces visually interesting.

glass act
Translucent glass above and below the white pendant shade provides a hint of color over the dining table.

weigh in
The dark floor adds weight to the bottom of the room and offers contrast to the white walls.

solid ground
The yellow pillow fabric combines with the white and patterned fabrics to reinforce the sunny vibe.

shady character
White wood shutters create dimension at the window but allow the patterned shades overhead to star.

Color clue
Plan to use bright, changeable accents to maintain interest in a quiet palette.

ATTRACT ATTENTION
A dominant color draws attention from ceiling to floor. Here, soft shades of yellow lead the eye from the lighting fixture to the artwork and painted chairs.

color mastery

Mixing drama with utility in the
dining room makes a statement about
you and the way you entertain.

FORMAL FASHION
Chair seats upholstered
in plush jewel-toned
fabrics match the deep
saturation of other colors
in the room.

Paint dining room walls in a hue that suits the time of day you use the space.

JAZZY ACCENTS
above right **Energize** neutral spaces with explosions of color on light shades, cushions, and tabletop accents.

ZESTY COLOR
above, far right **Colorful** accessories in fruity flavors connect pieces from disparate furniture styles. This busy corner looks open thanks to barely-there chairs.

DRAMATIC PAIRINGS
middle right **High-contrast** combos work beautifully in formal spaces when held in check with lush gray draperies and gray-painted woodwork.

ADD SOME PUNCH
middle, far right **Repeat** just one vibrant hue, such as this orange, to enhance streamlined schemes.

MORNING ROUTINE
right **Exuberant yellow is** an instant wake-up call and an ideal choice for a breakfast nook.

STAY CONNECTED
far right **Vivid green seats** echo the entry wall color, but partner with coral walls in this energy-infused dining room.

color mastery | continuous color

Bold hues and graphic patterns forge a visual link between no-borders dining and living spaces.

Indiana Clay

Olympic
Muted Fuchsia

Dark as Night

HIGH CONTRAST
above left **Highlight a tropics-bright scheme with strikingly massed splashes of black and white. Add pattern to a focal point wall using stencils; showcase photographs with white mats and black frames; and mix black-finished wood pieces with white slipcovered and upholstered chairs.**

SWAP PARTNERS
above **A dynamic duo fashions a dramatic union. Use pink and orange as accent colors, but switch the roles they play from room to room. Gauzy pink scarves on dining chairs link to the living room's chandelier and artwork, while tangerine throws on the living room chairs tie to the table linens.**

Color clue
Accentuate partial walls and deep-set windows with hot-hue paint.

LAYERS OF TEXTURE
left Take the chill off all that black and white with lush layers of tactile pleasures. Woven textiles and fresh flowers and foliage enhance the color story in the dining room, while slubby silk slipcovers and a shaggy rug increase textural interest in the living room. Heighten appeal by stacking framed photos or adding an oversize artwork, *opposite right,* created from stenciled and painted canvases.

pattern mastery

Your choice of patterns
and motifs will proclaim
your design style while
setting a relaxed or
rambunctious mood.

BALANCING ACT
Reiterate colors featured
in an eye-catching fabric
by adding solid, striped,
and small-to-medium-
pattern pillows and
upholstery fabrics.

Use a well-edited blend of patterns to serve up personality-plus dining rooms.

SPOTLIGHT SHAPES
above right **In a formal space, elegant motifs, such as this medallion, emphasize the backs of chairs sporting subtly solid-hue seats.**

THEMATIC PATTERNS
above, far right **Fashion a Far Eastern classic by covering walls in white-on-blue paper, laying a blue-and-red rug, and accessorizing with blue-and-white porcelain.**

GET COORDINATED
middle right **Link seating with color and pattern. A floral fabric on the chairs and pillows plays off the cushion's deep blue.**

STYLE FUSION
middle, far right **Pull together a stylistic pastiche with accent colors and patterns suggested by your collections.**

SPREAD SERENITY
right **Vary a dominant color's tone on accents, furnishings, and walls to create a quietly patterned palette that produces a peaceful easy feeling.**

COLOR GUIDE
far right **Breezy curtain panels inspire an informal, easy-on-the eye analogous palette.**

before & after

This thoughtful redesign focused on adding color, pattern, and purpose, turning a lackluster and underused dining room into a contemporary spot for eating and reading.

3 color fixes

1 Furnishings, draperies, and accents contribute pretty forms.

2 Rust-hue draperies and vine-pattern aquamarine wallpaper add noteworthy zing.

3 Plush chairs topped with damask pillows raise the warmth and comfort quotient.

BEFORE
3 color flaws

1 Perimeter voids create an unwelcoming space.

2 Blah colors and little pattern equals boring.

3 Hard chairs and table feel unwelcoming.

Turkish Coffee

Reynard

Sherwin-Williams
Reflecting Pool

Make it modern

Think enlightened and eclectic when establishing cutting-edge spaces.

Bold borders. Outfit walls with unexpected patterns presented in glorious color. This aquamarine paper boasts golden vines that introduce a botanical theme echoed by a pair of lamps. Dress windows in a complementary-hue solid fabric that frames the view.

Address the interior. A light-tone table accommodates dining, research, or kids' crafting. Surround it with streamlined seats done up in dark plush fabric. Carry the draperies' hues to the seating area with plump pillows in luxurious tone-on-tone fabric.

Stylish storage. Double-duty spaces require capacious caches. This sideboard's frosted-glass doors sound a modern note while making the multipurpose piece appear lighter on its feet.

Go with the classics. The weathered gilded mirror, iron drapery rods, family photos in wood frames, and white linen lampshades have withstood the style test of time.

NICELY NEUTRAL
A light-hue sisal rug anchors a contemporary collection of clean-lined furnishings sporting natural surfaces, a mix of light and dark finishes, and neutral upholstery.

STARRING ROLE
This kitchen shows how much impact colorful cabinetry can have. The seafoam color enhances the warm wall hue and brick flooring.

kitchens

Today's kitchens are meant for living, with room to gather as well as cook. When choosing colors, make this hardworking space an extension of your personal style.

Color strategies. CAREFUL CHOICES. Think about the building materials you covet most before choosing your kitchen's color palette. Start with the one that comes in the fewest options, such as a natural material. If you're dreaming of granite countertops, select the slabs before you order cabinet finishes and paint colors. CONTINUE A PALETTE. With today's more open floor plans, you'll want compatible colors in neighboring rooms. Treat your main communal rooms as one big gathering space and color accordingly. But compatible doesn't have to mean identical. Use darker or lighter versions of key colors in nearby rooms. Mix and match patterns and textures. COUNT ON CABINETS. Other than walls, cabinets offer the biggest blocks of space for creating colorful impressions. Select natural wood as a neutral foundation for brightly hued walls and dramatic floors. Or be adventurous and choose strong cabinet colors that command center stage. CHANGE PERCEPTIONS. Cool, pale walls make a small kitchen feel larger. Warm, dark hues add a sense of cozy comfort. Contrasting ceiling details—such as dentil molding or beams—draw the eye upward. A contrasting chair rail takes the eye around. TEXTURAL TOUCHES. Frame brightly painted cabinets in neutrals that create secondary interest with subtle patterns or textures: bas relief tiles, lightly veined stone, brushed stainless steel, wood species with distinct grains, or nubby window treatments.

try this combo

Inspired by 1940s dishware and a vintage range, this kitchen color scheme embraces a retro vibe and old-fashioned charm.

steel works
The gleam of metal chairs and appliances reflects light and offers a contrasting shine to the matte surfaces used throughout the room.

ties that bind
Goldenrod yellow ceramics echo the dominant hue in the adjacent family room, visually linking the spaces.

middle weight
A black finish on the island offers contrast to the white table and cabinetry and brings weight to the center of the room.

simple stripes
A restrained stripe of neutrals plus red adds pattern without competing with the vivid backsplash.

fancy footwork
The deep red linoleum flooring is durable and warm, providing a rich color base for the kitchen.

checkerboard
Eight colors of tile installed in a random pattern create a lively backdrop, which is set off by the white cabinetry.

visual links
The cornsilk-color countertop makes a visual bridge between the vivid hues and black and white cabinets.

Color clue
Add your floor
to the mix to
give you another
surface for a
swath of color.

FUN FACTOR
Multihue backsplash
tiles, retro appliances,
and kick-back casual
seating announce the
playful personality of
this kitchen redo.

color mastery

Forget about copying someone else's style. Pick colors that give a glimpse of your inner beauty.

TAILORED NEUTRALS
Give your kitchen a modern attitude by wrapping stainless-steel appliances in soft putty-color cabinets and tile. Woven shades, concrete countertops, and a checkered plywood floor add to the casual vibe.

Whether in the furniture, cabinets, floors, or walls, color gives your kitchen character.

ECLECTIC ENERGY
above right **Green barstools team with a gray countertop, brown cabinets, and sky blue walls to create an eclectic space for socializing.**

COTTAGE CHARM
above, far right **Classic white cabinets take on vintage airs when recessed door panels are painted a cheery yellow.**

TRENDY COMBO
middle right **Enliven the floor with multitone linoleum tiles, ceramic tiles, painted wood, or stained concrete.**

WOOD NOTES
middle, far right **The wood trim's orange tone plays a complementary partner to the blue cabinetry.**

TREND ALERT
right **If you want to try a trendy color, create a neutral foundation, then paint walls and some cabinets whatever color strikes your fancy.**

STATELY SURPRISE
far right **The crimson cabinetry in this kitchen changes the mood from formal to flirty.**

color mastery | making the grade

Connect your kitchen to the landscape by choosing a botanical bright to add life to sophisticated neutrals.

Bridgewood

Behr
Hidden Meadow

Milkyway Galaxy

WINDOW WOW

above left **A casual Roman shade uses its colorful stripes to link a black granite countertop and tiled backsplash with green and pale yellow painted cabinets. The small peninsula serves as both a bar area and part of a gracious transition from the colorful kitchen to the adjoining dining room done in quiet neutrals.**

NEUTRALS + GREEN

above **Celery green adds organic, life-affirming character to a lively kitchen decked out in black and buttery yellow with stainless-steel accents.**

BLACK BOUNDARIES

opposite **Black granite countertops and a black-painted beaded-board ceiling balance the zestiness of bright green cabinetry. Pale yellow cabinets and ceiling beams, plus an antique heart pine floor, act as an old-fashioned counterpoint to the modern stainless-steel touches.**

Paint power

Any hue can be created with paint. So think beyond the basic white or wood for your kitchen and pick colors that sing. Plan for longevity. The real cost of paint is in the labor. So before you splash on that trendy turquoise or spicy paprika, prep carefully to make paint last. Remove greasy residue. Fill in holes. Sand the surface smooth, then wipe clean. Use the proper primer. Now you're ready to paint. Use the best paint you can afford (the length of a paint's warranty is a good gauge for paint quality versus price), and add high-quality hardware to get the best look. Work with what you've got. Keep a band of upper cabinets from overwhelming a room by adding a few glass-front doors or painting an inset panel in a contrasting color. Paint window muntins in a color pulled from your window treatment fabric.

pattern mastery

Learn how to add another layer of style to your kitchen by mingling patterns that play well with cabinets and walls.

PATTERN PALETTE

above left **Help disparate fabrics seem like kissing cousins by choosing patterns with shared colors. Select the largest pattern first. Get bonus points for picking out a hue used elsewhere in the room—in this case, deep orange.**

NATURAL WONDERS

above right **A whimsical bird motif inspired this kitchen's homage to Mother Nature. The patterned fabrics partner with natural wood surfaces, sky-blue walls, and painted drawer panels on the island, creating a fun interplay of colors and patterns.**

EYE-CATCHING OUTLINES

opposite left **Repeat geometric shapes to create captivating patterns. In this room, circular plates, square tiles, and diamond-shape fretwork on cabinets and chairs help the eye move from one space to the next.**

FARMHOUSE FLAIR

opposite right **Show your guests the kitchen is meant for socializing by linking it to adjoining spaces with wallpaper. Using a vintage-style floral print creates a tea-stained country mood. The wallpaper does double duty here by also calling attention to handsome white ceiling beams.**

Sit back and relax

Today's kitchens are all about living. So soften those hardworking surfaces with patterns and pieces that draw people in. Express yourself. Raid your collections for beautiful pieces whose durable surfaces can withstand the heat, humidity, and spatters that come with cooking. Decorative tiles and collectible plates offer limitless patterns and colors. Shapely pieces of pottery create distinction when displayed against contrasting backgrounds. Warm it with wallpaper. Wallpaper works wonders when it comes to suggesting a style. Because kitchens are already busy places visually, keep patterns simple—such as the airy floral shown above right. Cover just one wall to get the benefits of a pretty pattern without making visitors feel closed in.

before & after

Going red takes nerve. But adding crimson cabinets—and a dramatic black-and-white floor—transforms a once-dull kitchen into a dynamic dazzler.

BEFORE
3 color flaws

1 Ho-hum white and neutral surfaces squelch any chance for personality.

2 The lack of natural light makes the room dingy.

3 Clustered accents and objects create visual clutter.

ENERGIZE WITH RED
above **Bold red cabinets and warm yellow walls change this kitchen's bland attitude. The black-and-white checkerboard floor offers a visual link to the kitchen's past.**

OUTLINE IN WHITE
left **Crisp white woodwork highlights striking architectural features— such as this arched display niche—against yellow walls.**

Gargoyle Shadow

Soft Terrain

Dutch Boy
Convivial Red

3 color fixes

1 Bright red cabinets and a black-and-white tile floor infuse the space with energy.

2 Yellow walls add artificial sunshine, while white subway tile reflects light into the room.

3 Colorful accents pack more punch with strategic placement around the room.

ACCENT WITH BLACK
Honed black-granite countertops rein in the room's energy while picking up the black trim on stainless-steel appliances.

Adding up the details

Simple changes create a kitchen filled with life.

Bright outlook. Spruce up cabinets with a warm paint color that explodes with energy—think red, orange, or intense yellow. Then choose fixtures—such as the retro pendants used here—to pick up on the dominant hue.

Rest the eye. Keep the countertops, backsplashes, and floor neutral to let hotter hues do their thing. Black, white, and stainless steel are obvious choices. But also consider gray, ivory, taupe, and natural wood tones as alternatives.

Add character. Throw in pops of color or contrasting textures to amp up interest. This kitchen gets part of its cheeky attitude from shiny glass knobs paired with satiny painted surfaces. Vibrant art pottery glows within solid-color niches.

Dressy details. Use glass-front cabinet doors or open shelves to show off colorful dishes. Store linens in shapely woven baskets. And soften your kitchen's hard edges with pretty upholstered chairs, woven shades, or colorful curtains.

COTTAGE COUTURE
A white-painted bed bursting with pillows in pink, green, and white conjures a cottage feel; floral motifs contribute to the breeziness.

bedrooms

Indulge yourself. Let your bedroom—the first room you see in the morning and the last one you see at night—reflect your unique aesthetic.

Color strategies. **UNIQUELY YOU.**
The bedroom is our private sanctuary from the outside world, the place we go to unwind and recharge, ready to face another day. Here are some ways to imbue a bedroom with a color personality that suits your lifestyle. **CREATING THE MOOD.** What do you want your room to reflect? Serenity or sauciness? Color will go a long way toward conveying that message. Muted hues (those hues with gray in them, such as dusty lavender, gunmetal blue, or sage green) whisper instead of shout and wash a room with quiet and calm. Clear colors (those without any gray, such as true red, kelly green, and juicy orange) speak loud and, well, clear. **FORM FOLLOWS FUNCTION.** How do you routinely use your bedroom? Do you keep a workstation on a desk for paying bills? Watch TV with the kids? Read quietly in a corner chaise? Keep it dedicated to restful sleep? Determining how you use your room and whether you share it with another person will help guide your palette choices and point you toward the ideal color intensity or level of saturation. **START WITH ONE BELOVED ITEM.** Maybe it's an heirloom bed, a fancy duvet cover, or fabric for curtains—whatever it is, if you love it, make it the foundation for the room's design. Choose elements that complement your treasure, then a few things that contrast harmoniously. Building off a single gorgeous piece ensures that the entire scheme is cohesive and meaningful to you personally.

try this combo

This master bedroom, with its many blues, tasteful reds, and quiet yellows, is neither overtly masculine nor feminine, so everyone feels at home.

tone on tone
A neutral ikat brings additional pattern to the bedding that coordinates, rather than matches.

unique batik
A tight, irregular batik pattern in tangy tomato red marches across a reversible coverlet that provides a contrasting layered look.

just the flax
Beige linen is a textural treat for lampshades and repeats on the chair cushion and bed pillows.

energetic footing
A woven rug of royal blue and white brings another blue into the room, along with a dynamic jolt of chevron pattern.

bench warmer
Ridged faille in gorgeous teal on the bench introduces a different blue into the scheme.

shady deal
Textured, barely-there window shades bring a hint of linear pattern that echoes the geometry found in other fabrics and accents.

plush and lush
Rich navy velvet wraps the back of an armchair in tactile decadence.

a touch of sun
The palest yellow paint coats the walls, tilting the room toward the warm side.

PRIMARY PALETTE
In this simple scheme built with relatively sedate primary colors, a playful mix of pattern adds jazzy personality.

color mastery

A successful scheme can consist of two hues or an entire rainbow. Whatever your preference, color will rejuvenate any bedroom.

COOL CHARACTER
Turquoise and white pack a powerful punch in this small room. Dabs of celadon green in the window treatments insert a second color.

Contrast is key. Pull in a few accessories that jump out against your main color.

GREEN SCHEME
above right **Stark contrasts between dark wood furniture and the lightest green walls give this room drama.**

PRETTY IN PURPLE
above, far right **A melange of dusky purples, from chalky lavender to aubergine, dress this bedroom in soothing, low-key elegance. Shots of gold and chartreuse provide the pop.**

BRIGHT DONE RIGHT
middle right **Ebony frames, paired with white walls and end tables, work with any accents. Here, orange and hot pink burst onto the scene.**

BLACK AND BLUE
middle, far right **Black and white create dramatic contrast. Baby blue walls are the cool counter to lipstick-red pillows.**

FRUIT FLAVORS
right **Lemon and lime juice up linens, while several shades of white tone down the bright flavor.**

A NEW NEUTRAL
far right **Pale blue works so effortlessly with dark wood, coral pillowcases, and an orange coverlet, it's practically a neutral.**

color mastery | calm quarters

In this restful room, warm beiges, browns, and blues come together for a contemplative mood, beckoning you to come in, put up your feet, and relax.

NEUTRALIZED
left A loose vine-print fabric dresses the French doors; its cream-and-brown combination echoes the neutral tones on the upholstered chair.

TWO BY TWO
above left A chalky blue coverlet sidles up to ivory and flax-hue pillows. Matching nightstands, lamps, and starburst mirrors flank the bed, supplementing the calm color palette with soothing symmetry.

GO FOR FAUX
above What looks like pale wood on the walls is actually wallpaper. Its warm tone and texture wrap the room and give a good base for darker brown, lighter cream, and dreamy blue.

Farrow & Ball
Joa's White

London Clay

Blue Ground

TAKE A SEAT

The seating area provides space for reading or quiet conversation. Pillows in muted yet playful patterns add personality. Tough, tan imitation-suede fabric covers the bench. You needn't choose only dark colors for fear of dirt or spills; this pale fabric is durable and releases stains. Or choose indoor-outdoor fabrics in a soft hand for pale colors that stand up to wear and frequent use.

pattern mastery

Bedrooms are a natural spot to pull in favorite motifs; the bed provides a perfect platform for a happy jumble of prints and patterns.

MESMERIZING MIX
Though this blend of bedding might appear random, its hues are all jewel tones (citrine, ruby, and amethyst), so they harmonize winningly.

Change the pattern scale (large, medium, and small) for the most dynamic design.

NEUTRAL BACKDROP
above right **The judicious use of pattern—green batik shams, aqua blue throw, and a pastel striped rug—pops against white elements.**

OFF THE WALL
above, far right **Solid sheets and bedding—interrupted only by monogrammed Zs—let the large, floral wallpaper take center stage.**

THREE-PEAT
middle right **If you're pattern shy, repeat one gorgeous fabric, such as this pale blue botanical, multiple times.**

BALANCING ACT
middle, far right **A single wall of striking pink paper stretches from floor to ceiling, balancing the complementary green plaid duvet and repeating the pink of the armchair.**

SUITE BLEND
right **A tumble of patterns—zigzags, florals, stripes—is tamed by two-tone blue walls and flirty white curtains.**

TWIST OF LEMON
far right **Celadon toile gets juiced up by a yellow leaf-print coverlet. Each pattern has an ivory ground in common.**

before & after

A bare bedroom—with only pale blue walls in its favor—becomes a heavenly haven hopping with lively pattern and zingy color.

BEFORE
3 color flaws

1 Pale blue walls were basically a blank slate.

2 The window was small and forgettable.

3 Flooring was old and worn.

Valspar *New Day*

Empire Fleet Blue

Crushed Cumin

Soft Skies

BREAK WITH BLUE
above Blue is the overwhelming favorite in this room, but it wouldn't shine so brightly without dashes of mustard yellow on the headboard and in the curtain fabric. Deep black furnishings give the zippy mix a bit of gravity.

CLEARLY CONVINCED
opposite The blues in this room mingle so well because they are all clear, saturated colors. White provides the ideal foil to keep all the colors crisply defined. Patterns play well together, too, ranging from large geometrics to a mix of florals within the simple color palette.

3 color fixes

1 Deep to light blues both energize and soothe.

2 Lush floral-pattern draperies highlight the window.

3 A striped blue rug pops against a freshly painted white floor.

All in the family
Selecting accent colors is easier than it looks.

Pick a card.
At your paint store, look at the color card with your wall color on it. The colors on each chip have the same value (the amount of pigment); the lighter colors simply have more white added. For a fail-proof accent color for your room, choose a lighter or darker color on the card. It's truly as easy as that.

Take another card.
To break out of the monochromatic habit, choose another color card in a complementary or analogous hue. Match the chip from your first accent choice to the color found in the same position on the second card and, voilà, the perfect color partner.

Let fabric guide you.
Look at a fabric you love that features your main color choice. Note the other colors in the pattern and the proportion of the hues. The two secondary hues used most are the accent colors to match.

Get professional help.
Turn to an online tool, such as *BHG.com/ editorscolorpicks*, to help guide your choice.

FOOD FOR THOUGHT
A colorful and light-filled room is a cheerful and stimulating space to encourage your child's intellectual and creative growth.

kids' rooms

Not just for getting ready for school or sleeping, kids' rooms are also places for playing, creating, dreaming, and storing all the special stuff that only children have.

Color strategies. BLOOMING COLOR.

It's easy to spot a child's bedroom as soon as you walk in the door. Kids' spaces are almost always more colorful than other rooms, and there's good reason: Children blossom when they're given permission to color, even if it's outside the lines. Try these ideas for planning a room that will nurture and inspire your child. **SOLICIT YOUR CHILD'S INPUT.** You may already know her favorite colors and motifs, but ask anyway; you may be surprised at what hues and features she wants in her room. She might also have innovative ideas for making homework and chores easier—you'll never know unless you ask! **CONSIDER TODAY AND THE FUTURE.** Dinosaurs may be all your son can think about at present,

but in a year or two, race cars may take the place of his beloved T. rex. Rather than going all out with a currently hot theme, introduce favorite items through accessories, such as lamps and pillows, which are easy to swap out when interests evolve. Include them as easily changeable elements rather than pricey furniture and flooring. **ROOM TO GROW.** A child needs attractive furnishings and storage just like adults do, so choose bookcases, cabinets, and shelves in neutral colors, such as wood tones, black, or white, that will harmonize with any decorating scheme and can adapt if your child changes her fancy. Use your budding artist's paintings and craft projects to bring color and an infusion of personality to the room.

try this combo

Cheery color and vibrant pattern bring just the right dose of whimsy into a boy's bedroom.

modern lines
A shiny brushed-stainless-steel bed frame brings in a smooth finish to balance the many tactile textiles in the room.

whirls and swirls
A single large pillow in a similar zany circle pattern sets the scheme for the rest of the bed, including a polka-dot throw at the foot.

earn your stripes
Bold stripes on a rug underfoot would echo the blue bands on the bedspread.

cool shades
Matchstick blinds in a medium wood hue complement the terra-cotta walls and filter harsh sun.

quiet carpet
Pale carpet just this side of beige is cuddly underfoot and provides a sound barrier in the room.

being green
Apple green is an eye-popping accent plucked from the rug; it appears on the bed as well as in the stuffed animals lounging on a shelf.

abundant blues
At least six shades of blue undulate on the bedcover; the lightest one was chosen for the sheets and pillowcases.

LITTLE BOY BLUE
Boys may insist on blue bedrooms, but don't let that limit the scheme. Tangy terra-cotta wall paint and zingy green accents shake up the blues.

color mastery

Use a child's favorite color as bold, eye-catching accents for a room that will please her now—and in the years to come.

A ROSE BY ANY NAME
Warm rose becomes downright elegant—and a touch exotic—when dabbed on sparingly. Tiffany blue and white temper its sweetness.

Draw color inspiration from anywhere: bedding, maps, rugs—even a child's artwork.

PRETTY IN PINK
above right **An abundance of pink is kept from sugar overload with off-white beds, an aqua nightstand, and dreamy artwork.**

WORLDLY EXPLOITS
above, far right **A giant map fills in for wallpaper in this bed alcove; its light blue and parchment hues are repeated in the bedding.**

MODERN MARVEL
middle right **A single pop of orange—in a midcentury rocker, no less—is the only color burst this modern room needs.**

ROCK 'N' ROLL
middle, far right **One complementary orange wall contrasts with navy blue bunk beds and highlights colorful accessories.**

POWERFUL PUNCH
right **Warm yellow bedding balances cool turquoise walls in this girl's room. A pink chandelier and red nightstand add zing.**

OLD-FASHIONED CHARM
far right **This golden-girl room is undeniably feminine, thanks to mustard-yellow toile coverlets, pleated shades, and warm white walls.**

pattern mastery

Mixing and matching suits children's exuberance and creativity, so throw caution to the wind when inviting colors and patterns into their rooms.

PINK POWER

left Pink's bolder sister, red, and green are opposites on the color wheel, so they have big impact when paired. A paler pink dresses the bed and windows for a break from the brightness. One large and vivid print limited to the two hues suffices in this color extravaganza. Other patterns remain tiny to avoid visual busyness.

BLUES ON THE GREEN

above left A girl's room doesn't have to be pink or purple—just take note of this winning combo of aqua and lime green. Floral patterns offer an element of femininity while polka dots and stripes increase the playfulness. A row of multicolor pennants marches around the room for additional accents.

EASY PATCHWORK

above A bed piled with a melange of linens takes on the look of a pieced-together quilt. Blue batik, pink polka dots, and red and blue stripes all make an appearance for a winning combination. The use of creamy taupe and antiqued-white furniture prevents the palette from veering into patriotic territory.

Color clue
Brighten a dark or dull room with sunny, warm hues.

UNEXPECTED COLOR
Autumnal tones of green, brown, and gold may be unusual in a child's room, but there's no denying they're cozy and perfect for a reading nook.

Kid-friendly color
Utilize these tips for drawing carefree color into a child's room.

Super saturated. We associate clear, saturated hues with children because kids themselves are often bold and fearless. If you—or your child—is a bit color shy, try a vibrant hue on just one wall or painted only to picture-rail (about two-thirds of the way to the ceiling) height.

Double your pleasure. Include two tints of the same color in a room for visual impact. Once you've chosen a favorite, such as pink, simply add white to it (for pale pink) or subtract white from it (for red).

Opposites attract. To make any color pop, choose its color-wheel counterpart as an accent. Blue rooms come alive with orange detailing; green rooms need a shot of red or pink for visual zip. Heart set on a purple room? Try yellow or gold accessories.

Having trouble? If you're short on ideas, look to a child's favorite artwork, book, or game for inspiration on a color, pattern, or motif.

before & after

A newly revamped room has lots of life in it for two school-age brothers who had outgrown their bunk beds and an old dresser.

BEFORE
3 color flaws

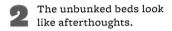

1 The deep blue walls are dark and claustrophobic.

2 The unbunked beds look like afterthoughts.

3 The changing-table-turned dresser needed a refresher.

CLEVER HEADBOARD
left Crafted from a new, solid pine door and painted gray-blue, the headboard picks up a color from the comforter and gives the beds prominence. Pillows in patterns of blue and orange plump up the bed.

PAINT TO THE RESCUE
above And not just any paint: chalkboard paint! A couple of coats on the old dresser and the new mirror make the pair look like a matched set—and the boys can draw and doodle to their hearts' content.

PLANNED PALETTE
opposite Dark khaki walls will wear well as the boys grow older. Colorfully striped bedding brings some crowd-pleasing blue back into the space while three, rather than two, hot orange curtain panels elevate the prominence of the pair of windows. As a warm complement to blue, the orange hue repeated through the room helps to balance the bold pattern on the beds.

3 color fixes

1 Dark khaki walls are warm and light.

2 Colorful headboards and striped comforters call attention to the beds.

3 Chalkboard paint and a hefty mirror revive the dresser.

Overcast   Classic Brown   Tangerine Dream

Pittsburgh Paints *Almond Cream*

Lime Green

The neutral zone

Every room—even vibrant kids' spaces—needs neutrals; they give the eye a spot to rest and keep other parts of the room from getting visually cluttered. Color foil. Many colors (maybe more than you think) are neutral and can be used to anchor a bold or heavily patterned scheme. Khaki walls, for example, serve just as khaki pants do in a wardrobe: as a goes-with-everything staple. It's warmer than white but not attention-seeking, the perfect background to a masculine room. Natural neutrals. Wood tones and the hues of natural grasses and plants play well with others, too. Matchstick shades, woven baskets, and grass rugs add texture as well as warmth. Black pepper. Black can have an important role in any room. In small doses, it gives visual weight to a piece of furniture without clamoring for attention. It outlines shapes and enhances colors. Many interior designers advise including a shot of black in every room for a dash of drama.

bathrooms

Not simply the utilitarian spaces of yesteryear, today's bathrooms can—and should!—have as much personality and color as a bedroom or kitchen.

Color strategies. PRACTICALLY PRETTY.

Perhaps the most practical room in a house, the bathroom is the place we get ready for work and prepare for rest after a long day. It's no wonder, then, that many homeowners seek bathrooms that possess the same colorful character as the rest of the house. Here's how to pull personality into this most private of rooms. **INTRODUCE COLOR WITH ACCENTS.** You don't have to embark on a major overhaul to incorporate new hues into a bath; you can simply bring in a fresh supply of bright towels, a rug, artwork for the walls, or a new soap dish and toothbrush jar. A coat of paint on the walls will usher in a new attitude, and because bathrooms are usually fairly small, such a change requires just a modest investment of time and money. **BE BOLDER WITH BIGGER CHANGES.** A bathroom that needs a refresher anyway is a good candidate for larger color upgrades. Tile, wallpaper, flooring, countertops, and light fixtures can showcase your personality and inject lively colors into the room. **LIGHT AND WHITE.** Light changes how we see color. The same hue will look very different in a bathroom with abundant sunshine than it will at night or in a windowless room. Test how your bath's light affects your favorite color throughout the day before committing to the hue. Remember that wall color can be reflected in white fixtures, hardware, and furnishings, changing their appearance.

try this combo

When the main elements—tile, fixtures, and walls—of a bathroom are white, you have license to invite in any color or pattern.

tiles with style
Small porcelain tiles provide subtle pattern. Vintage-look fixtures and tiles give a little bath charming character.

traditional toile
Covering walls with elegant pink-and-beige toile immediately imbues an all-white bathroom with charm and personality.

neutral, not boring
Natural elements, such as nubby baskets or a seagrass rug, anchor a room and bring warm texture to cold tile.

towel tones
Tantalizing in watermelon pink and lime green, terry cloth adds softness and visual texture.

perfect pair
Complementary red and green can be an eye-popping combo. Toning it down to pastel tints keeps them quiet.

BEGUILING BATH
In this mostly white bathroom, the color defines its character. Tea-stained toile, candy-hue towels, a striped rug, and sage furniture create a flirty ambience.

color mastery

For such a small room, it's amazing how many opportunities there are for adding color to the bathroom. Consider floor and wall tile, paint, towels, shower curtains, and accent pieces to slather your bath in defining hues.

GREAT PLANES
When everything else is neutral, great planes of saturated color, plus a pale wood tone and metal elements, stand out elegantly.

Keep bath cabinetry and fixtures neutral; show your colors on walls and accessories.

CABINET CONTRAST
above right **Flat-door cabinets with a red tone play off walls sheathed in green-tinged tiles.**

SUNNY DISPOSITION
above, far right **Cheery yellow paint washes the walls of a white bath with just a hint of sunny color.**

BUTTONED-UP BEAUTY
middle right **Gray floor-to-ceiling tiles, a gleaming mirror, and the black, white, and acrylic chair soak this bath in glamour.**

PURPLE REIGNS
middle, far right **Dark cherry cabinetry and plum-painted walls simmer with red undertones.**

GLOBE TROTTING
right **Deep, rich earth tones of mahogany, pumpkin, and ebony with dashes of the exotic give this room a global vibe.**

PEACHY KEEN
far right **Apricot walls and a pink vanity pick up hues from the tossed-blossom shower curtain. Sage green accessories are a natural complement to flowery colors. White wainscoting and fixtures provide the neutral foil.**

color mastery | details

It's the little things that can make or break a bathroom. Give those details, the elements easily overlooked, the full chance to shine.

FLOWER POWER

above **What could have been just a ho-hum, tiled niche for shampoo and soap blossoms with a bit of creativity and lemon-yellow tile.**

TERRIFIC TRANSITION

avove right **Treating a wall of tile like a painted or papered wall—with one color on the bottom, another on top, and a band of molding between them—dresses up this bathroom. A random mix of blues and greens in the accent tiles is a whimsical touch.**

A PERFECT FIT

opposite left **A tiny bath, where every element fits just so, is the right spot for a splash of color or drama. Shapely blue floor tiles, a glossy black door, gray-veined marble wall tiles, and a brass sconce amp up the sophistication.**

FOLLOW THE LINES

opposite right **Picking out the decorative molding in this small bath takes the simple French blue and opalescent gray color palette to a new level of sophistication.**

Big style in a small space

Because bathrooms are usually small, indulging in fancy finishes and specialty surfaces is financially doable—you'll need only a few square yards of any material, after all—and it adds architecture to an otherwise featureless room. **Start with walls.** Paneling, tile, woodwork, mirrors, and even wallcoverings (if rated for a high-humidity environment) invigorate a plain, boxy bath, especially when these elements are vibrant with color. Powder rooms offer more options for wallcoverings since humidity is generally not an issue. These small spaces are also ideal for trying out trendy or vibrant colors. **Look to the ceiling.** Many designers call this a room's fifth wall with good reason. It too can be a canvas for paint, molding, tiles (think copper or tin), or wallpaper—and it doesn't have to match the rest of the room. A contrasting ceiling might be just what a small space needs. If it suits your style, add the glitter of a chandelier for extra sparkle.

pattern mastery

Bring pattern into the bath with multiple materials. Use mosaic tiles, mottled stone, printed fabrics, and flecked finishes.

CATCH THE WAVE
A giant painting of a crashing wave stirs excitement in this master bath. An armchair upholstered in undulating stripes and flooring that looks like raindrops on a pond's surface reinforce the watery theme.

Play with scale. Large patterns can be dynamic additions to a small bathroom.

TWO'S COMPANY
above right **This celadon-and-white palette is simple, but patterns in varying scales stave off boredom.**

A BIT OF BLUE
above, far right **Floral wallpaper in two shades of turquoise, which repeat in the curtain trim and vanity knobs, provides all the color this mostly white room needs.**

A TAILORED FIT
middle right **Gray mosaic tiles hemmed in by thin stripes take on the look of a menswear plaid. Bold checkered flooring plays with scale.**

JUNGLE FEVER
middle, far right **A chartreuse wallcovering in a huge leaf pattern instantly warms this modern bath.**

VINTAGE DELIGHT
right **A wide border of blue and green mosaic tiles spins off the Tiffany-blue wall color and slightly lighter blue vanity.**

BLACK AND WHITE
far right **With a classic black-and-white palette, you can layer on pattern. Plaid and toile cover every inch of this bath.**

before & after

Here comes the sun! Once wan and charmless, this vintage bathroom cheered right up with cozy wall paint and an eye-catching window shade.

BEFORE
3 color flaws

1 Mostly white wallpaper was almost invisible.

2 The curtains were filmy and flimsy.

3 Lack of color made the black tile stripe the only interesting feature.

ALL RIGHT WHITE
above **The vintage white wall tile and black floor tiles were in good shape and didn't need replacement, so the color fix was relatively inexpensive. Rich yellow paint is now the perfect backdrop for white stenciling that adds a touch of elegance.**

CLEAN AND CRISP
left and opposite **Because the tile is mostly white with black accents— including a sharp pinstripe that wraps around the room—those colors were repeated in the shelf niche and the framed artwork.**

AFTER
3 color fixes

1 Yellow paint contrasts beautifully with the black and white tile.

2 A rust-color fabric shade in a tight pattern dresses the window.

3 Stenciled white damask motifs add interest to the yellow walls.

True Value
Chinese Mustard

Kumquat

SKIRTING THE ISSUE
left Concealing the sink's pipes with a prim white skirt—tied just so with rust-hue ribbons—provides a clean look. More rust-color details, such as the upholstered stool and the window shade, offer the right dose of contrast.

WARM WINDS
Imbue a porch with color and comfort. Patterned pillows add character, while brown-and-black striped panels offer warmth and privacy.

porches

Think of this outdoor living room as a friendly smile on your house's facade that's ready to greet visitors and invite them in to sit a spell.

Color strategies. EXTENDED
LIVING. Because porches extend a home's living space, they boast the best of both worlds: the coziness of an interior room with the breezy ease of the great outdoors. Likewise, color cues can come from inside your home or from Mother Nature—whose mastery of mixing hues is unmatched. Consider these ideas when planning your perfect porch. **PLAY HOUSE.** A porch's palette should complement hard-to-change elements of a home's facade, such as brick, stone, or exterior paint colors. If the house's coloring is already bold, the porch should not compete. If the house itself is neutral, you can opt for more punch on the porch. **FABRIC FILL.** Today's outdoor-grade fabrics rival their inside-only counterparts in style but are waterproof and durable—and they introduce pattern and color on a porch in a snap. Curtains, cushions, and pillows will soften hard edges and enliven furnishings. **WHEN IN DOUBT, GO GREEN.** All greens go together and mix with any color—just look at your landscape for proof and inspiration—so green will look right at home in this outdoor room. **TRANSFORM WITH PAINT.** You can unify the most motley crew of mismatched furniture with a coat or two of outdoor spray paint; when properly applied, it'll even allow an indoor chair or table to endure the elements on a porch. Painting a piece rich black will ground an arrangement, while crisp white paint will lighten it.

try this combo

Create a seaside cottage attitude with crisp white pieces emboldened by a bucket of blues and pops of green.

deep impact
Bold blue fabric on the swing catches the eye and anchors the whole arrangement.

a swirl of flowers
A large-scale floral doesn't overwhelm, thanks to a neutral background and small doses, such as on pillows.

natural beauty
A rough-woven rug in hardy sisal warms up all the blues and whites.

paisley power
Swirling paisley fabric in a storm of blues revives tired chair cushions. Cobalt piping sharpens the edges.

walk on the beach
Bountiful blues and beiges evoke water, sand, sky, and a breezy outlook.

CAPTIVATING COMBO
Blue and white is a favorite color combination for a porch. Seafoam green and nubby tan keep the scheme from going cold.

Color clue
Accentuate the outdoor connection with foliage colors from chartreuse to blue-green.

SEALS & SEA LIONS
A PORTRAIT OF THE ANIMAL WORLD

color mastery

Use the pleasure pursuits of warm weather, such as a walk on the beach or a stroll to the ice cream parlor, to inspire color choices for your porch.

BREATH OF SPRING
Textiles in pink and yellow with pops of green and peach shine as this porch's main stars, while white furniture and a pale blue floor are the supporting cast.

Pick a porch palette that complements the style and architecture of your home.

CUTE COTTAGE

above right **A table and chairs in wood-tone bamboo bring warmth to periwinkle cushions and a pale green cabinet and light fixture.**

AT THE LODGE

above, far right **A pastel green sofa and blue and chartreuse pillows are lighthearted contrasts to black furniture and rustic stonework.**

FRUIT PUNCH

middle right **Saturated hues in fruity colors of orange, lemon, and pomegranate create a warm and playful palette. Touches of green and blue cool things down.**

OPPOSITES ATTRACT

middle, far right **Turquoise chairs, cushioned with pillows in tangerine—its color-wheel counterpart— engage the eye.**

BY THE SEA

right **Seaglass-blue walls, a striped rug, and white wicker get a jolt with a lime green glider and orange accents.**

TACTILE PLEASURES

far right **Textured woven furniture is a delight to see and to touch; it holds its own against the patterned cushions and aqua pillows.**

pattern mastery

Homeowners need not fear loud prints and cacophonous combinations. An open-air porch is one place where layers of pattern will dazzle.

YIPES, STRIPES!
left Stripes and plaids are a safe way to wade into waves of pattern; here, they jazz up white armchairs and inject a splash of color.

PRINTS CHARMING
above left A matched set of furnishings with the same flax-color upholstery is a sure-footed background for pillows and throws in wild hues, from saucy pink to lime green.

WHITE AND WILD
above Walls and furniture in white and wood tones allow a concert of prints to sing joyously. Orange, green, yellow, and purple join in the harmony. The mix of prints works because the colors are all balanced in intensity. Overhead, paper lanterns take solid color up to the ceiling.

TROPICAL RESPITE

left Exotic splashes of orange, pink, and yellow are tempered by linen-beige and white, which become a restful place for the eye among the bold and busy patterns.

before & after

A barren and underused porch springs to life with a cozy swing, cushy rugs, and a color scheme inspired by autumn leaves.

BEFORE
3 color flaws

1 Concrete flooring was drab underfoot.

2 A lack of furnishings was uninviting.

3 The porch palette was dark and dreary.

Kelly-Moore Paints
Chimenea

Alligator Alley

Sky Watch

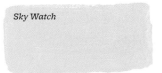

HARVEST HUES
above **The brick facade— a rich rust color—is reminiscent of fall, sparking the porch's whole color scheme of gold, orange, and sage green. Pale blue accents are a pleasing, cool contrast to all the warmth.**

AN EASY APPROACH
opposite **All who bound up the steps now are greeted by wood decking softened by seagrass rugs in green, orange, and blue. Rocking chairs, side tables that resemble tree stumps, and a rolling coffee table cluster around a charming swing piled with pillows.**

AFTER
3 color fixes

1 Durable ipe wood planks lend a gorgeous golden hue.

2 Furnishings with kick-back comfort invite long chats on the porch.

3 Vivid and cheery colors brighten the space.

DECORATING Elizabeth Mayhew

colin cowie chic

think COLOR GUILD

add color in stages

If you want to change your palette
over time, follow our step-by-step ideas
for introducing layers of color in
easy increments.

artistically inspired

A ho-hum living room gets a high-powered makeover in easy steps when artwork inspires juicy-hue walls and an infusion of colorful accents and textiles.

1

SEATING SLUMP

This living room has good bones—great shuttered windows, a light wood floor, and ample proportions. But the neutral furnishings offer little interest against pale gray walls. The large pieces in the main grouping, though comfy, don't relate well to each other or offer a welcoming vibe. The corner seating group feels disconnected.

Sherwin-Williams
Grassland

Rugged Brown

2
START WITH ART

Two new works of art provide the colorful inspiration this room needs. The charming area rug repeats the mustard yellow in the botanical-themed painting on the large wall, bringing instant playfulness and warmth to the space. In the corner, an abstract landscape repeats the golden notes along with bands of blue and rust that inspire zesty-hued pillows and accents.

Sherwin-Williams
Grassland

Rugged Brown

Solaria

artistically inspired

The key to this makeover's success is a design plan that mixes color, pattern, and texture in a cohesive look.

reach out
Textural maize pillow covers repeat the wing chair fabric color across the room.

color play
Figural pillows are playful and pull all the colors of the room together in one lively pattern.

card game
Paint chip cards featuring color matches for hues in the artwork provide the clues for choosing wall and accent colors.

worth repeating
Petal pillows pick up the gray from the walls and artwork while also adding dimensional texture.

depth of interest
A dimensional green pillow repeats the wall and ottoman color on the sofa and echoes the texture and shapes on the rug.

carry through
A geometric print on the side chairs brings out the khaki and ecru found in the textured sofa fabric.

energy bars
Zigzag bands of color bring light and movement to the solid sofas.

patch of green
Mottled green leather repeats the brown sofa finish with the addition of vibrant color.

understated
Yellow loses its brown undertones and takes on a softer pastel tint in the corner seating.

keep it quiet
An interlocking geometric pattern provides softness at the windows in the form of relaxed shades.

build a bridge
Shades of brown, tan, and ecru mix in the sofa fabric, creating a bridge between the dark and light colors in the room.

3

WOW WITH WALLS

Accent walls painted in chartreuse and rust provide visual punch to this now warm and inviting living room. The brown leather sofa moves away from the wall to provide a physical break from the adjacent dining room. A green leather ottoman provides a focus for the furnishings, which are punctuated with pops of color and pattern. Adding lightness in the corner, the classic wing chairs are replaced by modern versions in maize, while a striped rug echoes the bands of color in the artwork that ties back to the rest of the room palette.

Sherwin-Williams
Copper Mountain

Solaria

Sands of Time

Antiquity

accessorize with color

Adding colorful details bit by bit takes these rooms from pale to perky, proving that serene spaces can handle bold color without losing a soothing personality.

Pittsburgh Paints
Almond Roca

1
NEUTRAL START
A linen-color table and chairs make an elegant set but offer little visual contrast to the bare wood dining room floor. A scrubbed pine sideboard, bamboo frame mirror, and vintage chandelier provide quiet notes of neutral texture.

Pittsburgh Paints
Almond Roca

Golden Cricket

Orange Liqueur

2
SHADES OF COLOR
A dash of color and a pinch of pattern freshen the dining room with an area rug in apple green. Sculptural floor lamps with orange silk shades flank the sideboard. Additional doses of color come from the candles and glass containers filled with limes and oranges.

3

PLAYFUL PALETTE

The room gets an infusion of warm pink inspired by the bouquet of hydrangeas on the table. Green curtain panels in a trellis pattern build on the garden theme planted by the modern floral-print pillows. A large painted canvas adds color to the white walls.

Pittsburgh Paints
Almond Roca

Golden Cricket

Orange Liqueur

Rose Glory

accessorize with color

Kelly-Moore Paints
Timothy Tan

1 BLANK SLATE

Beige walls, painted white case goods, and creamy indoor/outdoor upholstery fabric make this living room comfortable but bland. The well-placed arrangement and the assortment of neutral textures make a good base to start adding changeable color with vibrant accent pieces.

2 EASY ADDITIONS

Bold splashes of orange and red add zest to the room. The sinuous lines of the graphic red-and-white organic-pattern rug balance the rigid stripes on the curtain panels. A lacquered orange cube table, red artwork, and red pillows add visual punch.

Kelly-Moore Paints
Timothy Tan

Matthew's Fire

Red Baron

3

SATURATION POINT

Sassy accents in red, orange, and green pump up the energy level. Red striped curtains take color to the walls while painted red side tables ground the armless sofa. A stacked-ball lamp topped with a luscious orange shade adds curves.

Kelly-Moore Paints
Timothy Tan

Matthew's Fire

Frog Prince

Red Baron

the power of paint

This three-step makeover turns a blah, beige living room into a space for family and friends to relax, unwind, and spend quality time together.

True Value
Sympathy

1

UNINSPIRED
With an abundance of natural light, this area cries out for a well-coordinated work space instead of an inadequate hand-me-down table with a worn finish and impersonal color palette.

True Value
Familiarize

Maui Sunset

2

GETTING IT TOGETHER
Multicolor striped drapery panels bring color and softness to this corner of the room. A pair of dove gray file cabinets organizes clutter and supports a scrap piece of countertop material to fashion a do-it-yourself desk. Baskets and pale blue linen-covered binders bring in tonal texture.

3
RIGHT ON TRACK

The office space is now pretty and productive. A built-in desktop and shelving play the warmth of wood against a brick-color accent wall. Overhead, a style-savvy pendant lends a punch of personality to this all-business space.

True Value
Familiarize

Maui Sunset

Motivation

Lucky Penny

the power of paint

Better Homes and Gardens
Creamy Pebbles

Fiery Red

1
LACK LUSTER
With beige walls, comfy—but brown— furniture, and few accessories, this living space doesn't offer much in the way of color or pattern. But with a lovely set of French doors, beautiful wood floors, and a traditional mantel flanked by windows, it has the potential to become the family's favorite room.

2
COLORFUL POTENTIAL
Striped drapery panels frame the large windows and mantel in an upbeat tempo. A botanical rug anchors the sofa in the center of the room. Throw pillows break up the sectional's neutral upholstery with pops of bright color that echo hues in the artwork.

Better Homes and Gardens
Creamy Pebbles

Fiery Red

Blue Drop

Better Homes and Gardens
Creamy Pebbles

Blue Drop

Fiery Red

Copper Pipe

3

LIVELY FAMILY RETREAT A playful paint palette of warm brick and cool blue borrows hues from the striped drapery panels and gives the room a delightful backdrop for the neutral woods and upholstery. An abundance of colorful pillows on the sectional adds color and pattern to the center of the room. On the windows, relaxed Roman shades provide another layer of softness, while striped panels set off the French doors.

fabulous fabrics

A three-step makeover amps up the luxury in this dining room by expanding the neutral palette with rich, textural fabrics.

1

SIMPLY STAID

A palette of beige, off-white, and brown plays it too safe in this space. The bland pallor doesn't highlight the impressive architecture or allow any particular element to shine. The china collection on display as well as the Roman shades hint at a fashionable color scheme that could easily come to life.

Ace Paint
Ivory Pearl

2
PALETTE POTENTIAL
Colors in the china inspire a palette of purple and green. Purple scallops trim the Roman shades; pillows and a rug add color on the banquette and floor. A green leather settee makes a bold style statement.

Ace Paint
Ivory Pearl

Twine

3

TASTEFULLY REFINED

Slipcovers dress the chairs in purple velvet trimmed in beaded fringe and coordinating fabric, infusing the room with warmth. Drapery panels in a silk stripe add texture and softness to the window bay. A background of green in the shelving units makes the china collection pop, while molding-framed wallpaper does the same for a green leather settee on the wall opposite the sideboard.

Ace Paint
Ivory Pearl

Twine

Council Oaks

Historic Charm

Color clue
Frame a botanical-
motif wallpaper to
mimic a view on a
windowless wall.

color with character

Every woman deserves a little glamour in her life. See this architecturally bland boudoir shift from drab to dreamy in three easy steps.

1
BEIGE AND BASIC
The mood of this suite is tasteful but devoid of warmth or character. While neutral is not a naughty word in the bedroom, accessories and pillows in rosy pink and effervescent orange tones provide a tantalizing taste of what this room could become.

Olympic
Crescent Moon

Peachy Keen

2
GLAM BEGINNINGS

In a room lacking architectural detail, character comes from color and pattern. A rosy taupe wall color instills warmth and intimacy, while flirty touches such as the ornate mirror frame and shell chandelier deliver a big dose of glamour. Plaid slipcovers inject tone and texture in the seating area, while pillows and a throw enliven the bedding.

Olympic
Crescent Moon

Peachy Keen

Arabian Sands

color with character

Olympic
Arabian Sands

Peachy Keen

Cranapple

Crescent Moon

3
SUPER SUITE

Color imbues the room with cheerful character thanks to silk taffeta panels framing the windows and closet doors. The vanity nook strikes a dramatic pose with the definition of a delightful butterfly-pattern wallpaper. The tri-color drawer unit that inspired the palette moves to center stage here. On the bed, an exquisite duvet blushes with shades of pink, while a coat of tangerine awakens the closet wall. Lime throw pillows in the sitting area introduce a pleasing new dimension to the vivid orange-and-pink scheme.

Color clue
In the bedroom especially, it's important to use colors that make you feel at ease.

Phase-to-phase color

Approach your color makeover in simple steps to create a winning combination.

Gather ideas. Over time, save samples of fabrics and wallpapers you love. Tear out magazine pages that inspire you. Pick up paint chips and add to the mix to get an idea of where your color heart lies.

Take inventory. Review what you have to work with—in the room, in another, or in storage—and what may be modified to suit your color preferences.

Choose your mood. Determine the feeling you want your room to invoke. This will help you choose color values and intensities. Consider how you use the room, at what time of day, and who spends the most time there.

Create a balance. Decide which color will dominate about 60–70 percent of your room (the walls or cabinetry), which color will cover 20–30 percent of the room (usually window treatments, rugs, and upholstery), and which color will enhance the 10 percent represented by accent pieces.

seasonal sensations

If the most interesting element of a deck is the railing, it's time to make a change. Watch this uninspiring space take on colorful personality in three easy steps.

Behr
Canyon Cloud

1
UNINVITING AURA

An unadorned iron chaise takes up a corner on the deck that would be better used as an alfresco dining space. Although the lattice railing provides a measure of privacy, the view of the trash cans and air-conditioning unit leaves something to be desired.

Behr
Canyon Cloud

Chocolate Coco

Winter Hedge

2
WEAVE IN TEXTURE

A bistro table and chairs set featuring modern lines replaces the chaise. The woven look complements the seating inside on the porch (shown on page 178). A potted tree separates the deck from its surroundings and adds much-needed foliage color.

Color clue

Coordinate your deck and porch plantings just as you do for room accents inside.

3

SUMMERTIME FLAIR

The deck gets a splash of color from a bright green chair in a branchlike pattern. Flowers, plants, and trees surround the seating, creating intimacy and blocking signs that the rest of the neighborhood is just a few feet away.

Behr
Winter Hedge

Carolina Parakeet

Chocolate Coco

Bliss Blue

soft summer classic

A drab screen porch transforms into a fabulous retreat thanks to a colorful mix of durable and comfy furnishings.

Valspar
Very Black

Clear Blue Sky

Garden Fresh

1 BARE MINIMUM

A color palette of lime green and turquoise is a summer classic, but there is too little of it to make a playful impact in this space. The bench cushion is a good starting point, but the room needs more soft elements and potted plants to tie it to the view and make it a comfy retreat.

Valspar
Gardener's Soil

Well Water

Green Tea

2 ADDED COMFORT

Seating moves to a cozy corner with a synthetic woven sectional. Lime green and turquoise pillows in fade-resistant outdoor fabrics add a dose of color to the off-white covers on the deep cushions and begin to build the palette. Plants and flowers add eye-catching color and shape to the coffee table.

Valspar
Gardener's Soil

Green Tea

Well Water

Ocean Sigh

3

COLOR AND STYLE

Modular furniture in bold hues gives this space versatility and a color boost. Four ceramic tables in bright turquoise and lime green push together to create one large coffee table. The woven table reports to the end of the sectional for side-table duty. A graphic patterned rug and plethora of colorful pillows create soft landings everywhere, while plantings brighten every surface. Creamy curtain panels banded in contrasting brown control the intensity of light in the porch.

color through the house

Learn how to create a connected color scheme that unites every room in your home.

pattern play

powerful palette

Noted Arkansas designer Tobi Fairley revels in pumped-up hues and patterns. Her colorful signature repeats throughout this Little Rock abode.

In Tobi Fairley's circa-1976 home, which she shares with her husband, Carter, and daughter, Ellison, peppy palettes flow from the black-and-white entry to the kelly green living room to the family room, where black and green meld with orange. "To live with me, you have to love color," Tobi says. This master of the mix shares the following tips for creating personality-plus spaces:

Curb your enthusiasm. Don't put all your favorite hues and patterns in a single room. Successful designs are the most edited rooms, so after you've decorated a space, take out at least one vibrant object.

Vary the value. Mix just two or three energetic accent colors with one or two neutrals. Layer different values of these hues in patterns of various scales to keep a room from looking too busy.

Make cohesive connections. Use different color palettes in different areas of your home, but tie rooms together by repeating a color and employing similar patterns or patterns sharing the same background hue.

GRAPHIC GROUNDING
Black backdrops and ebony accents anchor high-powered color schemes that feature strong patterns.

> "When both patterns and colors are bold, use less of each so as not to overpower a room."
>
> —**Tobi Fairley,** homeowner and interior designer

Glidden
Arizona Sunset

Leapfrog

Equinox

Manuscript

ARTISTICALLY ALLOCATED

above left **Minimize motifs in often-used rooms to generate calm. Start with neutral walls, floor, and furniture before adding wow-power colors and textures. Lime green— placed as a shiny lampshade, a sculptural urn, a woven throw, and the background on the bookcases—brightens without overpowering the family room's laid-back vibe.**

STIMULATE SENSES

above **Citrus zest is introduced in attention-grabbing ways. Luscious oranges—ranging in tone from sherbet-hue lamps and Far Eastern-flavor throw pillows (***previous page***) to a tangerine wing chair embellished with a white medallion and welting and a lacquered bench—make refreshingly fetching partners for lime green.**

CLEVERLY COMBINED
Traditional takes a turn by dressing classic furnishings in avant-garde pairings. Chair backs in flowery fabric partner with kiwi-color vinyl to fashion sophisticated seats.

REFLECT & RELATE
Mirror fabric patterns in unexpected ways. The table boasts a Greek-key design that references the wing chairs' shapely geometric motifs.

Color clue
Buff walls highlight lively furnishings and gilded surfaces.

EQUAL WEIGHT
White consoles and a raw-silk-covered sofa create a united composition, while wing chairs, lamps, and striped pillows present weighty splashes of green.

Ralph Lauren Paint
Cameo

Track Green

Limeade Green

Chrome

Stage a color reverse
You can achieve a dynamic look with a limited range of colors and the right mix of fabrics. Two-tone twist. A monochromatic or two-tone scheme can read as the polar opposite of monotonous by using a shift of color dominance. Reversing patterns from color on white to white on color keeps the look light on its feet. Mixing motifs. Oversize motifs paired with narrow stripes or small prints introduce the tension of opposing scales. Sinuous botanical patterns counterpoint angular geometrics, while figural patterns animate the space.

KEEP IT SIMPLE
above When working with boldly patterned wallpaper, simplify the rest. Display single-image artwork in gilded frames, and choose clean-lined accents and furnishings that echo wall colors.

ESTABLISH CALM
above middle In the kitchen, Tobi opted for all-white serenity that puts the focus on the fruits of her culinary labors.

FASHION FUSION
above right High-contrast wallpaper creates a lively transitional space in the entry. The botanical motif relates the paper to patterns used in adjacent rooms, making a clear visual connection.

MAKE COPIES
right The botanical forms, a striped rug, the houndstooth banquette, and chalkboard doors allude to colors and motifs used elsewhere in the home.

"I enjoy using colors that trends say are out. When people say teal or burgundy are done, I like to prove them wrong."
–**Tobi Fairley,** homeowner and interior designer

STUNNING SCENE
This bedroom gets its drama from a striking color trio, a stunning pictorial fabric, and the use of stripes in two sizes.

boldly bohemian

Saturated shades—long employed to enrich formal interiors—take a turn toward hip, generating drama in contemporary and classic homes.

The owners of this 1910 Victorian abode used jewel tones to fuse their modern aesthetic with the home's historic bones. The posh palette creates distinctive looks, from lighthearted to luxuriant. Though suited to most design styles, jewel tones require thoughtful placement. Maximize the colors' impact by:

Finding a muse. Draw your palette from multicolor accessories. Seek inspiration from an oversize artwork or patterned fabric that suits your style. Pick three or four colors to repeat throughout your home.

Spotlighting properly. These intense colors deserve a center-stage position. Think very light or very dark when choosing restful backdrops for these colors; if you set them against medium-tone backgrounds, the results will be muddied.

Mixing temperatures. Meld cool tones, such as peacock and aquamarine blues and jade greens, with warmer topazes, carnelian oranges, and citrusy yellows and limes to create perfectly pleasing blends.

**POINT,
COUNTERPOINT**
Whimsically patterned
pillows and unexpected
animal prints
contemporize these
classic furniture pieces.

FINELY FINISHED

opposite Contemporary prints and gem-tone colors on accents bring a modern atmosphere to this Victorian home. Clean-lined furniture in neutral hues confirms the contemporary aesthetic. Shimmering pale turquoise draperies add a note of decadent luxury.

RETHINK RATIOS

above Switch the roles of dominant and secondary hues from room to room. Various colors appear in nearly equal quantities in the living room while aubergine moves to the forefront in the dining room. The deep purple pops on an upholstered bench and walls that highlight burnt orange draperies.

STAGED SURPRISES

above right Emphasize color connections and captivate the eye with compositions that provide a spark of contrast. Here, dark walls and a neutral runner spotlight glassware, hydrangeas, and a vase that mirror the green, blue, and lilac shades outfitting the nearby living room.

Like a lower-contrast look? Paint ceilings light gray or tan to tone down the transition between vertical and horizontal spaces.

Up to Date

Fresh Orange

Maryann

Ace Paint
Ohio Buckeye

STREAMLINE SHAPES
above left **These homeowners carried their favorite dark wood finishes and pared-down silhouettes into the kitchen. Home-center cabinets updated with custom cornices and modern hardware complement the blue walls and shimmering mosaic-tile backsplash.**

COLOR COORDINATE
above **Banish workaday worries by outfitting utilitarian spaces with vibrantly hued cooking gear and graphic area rugs. If you find it hard to match precious-stone colors, opt for brightened-up versions. Cheerful accessories are welcome additions in any kitchen.**

LUSHLY LAYER
opposite **Build neutral backdrops to spotlight your snappy scheme. Amplify understated interest by arranging multiple textures in varying tones at different levels. In this master bedroom, chocolate walls and a beige cornice board highlight straw-gold draperies, which in turn accentuate the tawny upholstered headboard.**

Color clue
Juice up jewel tones by adding citrus-green and lemon yellow accessories.

Razzle dazzle

Turn to these tried-and-true techniques for updating interiors with fabulous and fashionable jewel tones.

Vary views.
Gemstone paints highlight a room's assets, camouflage its flaws, and increase a room's coziness quotient. Opt for eggshell finishes—the slightly shiny sheen shows jewel hues to their best advantage.

Be cool.
Fashion serene quarters by introducing white. The cool hue sounds a calming note, gives the eye a place to rest, and nicely balances the boldness of these color-rich tones.

Maximize motifs.
Ply patterns with precision to create harmonious spaces. Slot in plenty of plain fabrics and neutrally patterned accents that put jewel-tone elements solidly in the limelight.

Glam it up.
Reflect jewel tones' inherent richness by including elegantly shaped lamps, chic chandeliers, refined furniture, silky textiles, upholstered headboards, and cornices.

strategy shift

Once fearful of color, owners of this Sag Harbor, New York, cottage now embrace streamlined interiors linked by pumped-up hues and progressive patterns.

Designer Tara Seawright eased her clients into color by creating high-impact designs requiring minimal-to-moderate investment. "We introduced color using pillows, throws, bed linens, and ceiling paint," Seawright says. "We used things that weren't a big commitment and that could easily be changed." To create quick-change connections, Seawright advises:

Start with neutrals. Opt for simple fabrics; dress windows with wood blinds; paint walls white; and remember that animal prints work as neutrals.

Tie it together. Here, oranges, hot pinks, yellows, browns, animal prints, 1960s silhouettes, metal finishes, and whimsical nautical and natural motifs link spaces.

Test-drive accessories. Buy pillows and accents and group them, on a sofa or tabletop, to see how they partner. Don't like the look? Return them and try again.

Intensify interest. Invest in neutral-hue pieces sporting fluffy, shimmering, stony, and woven textures to heighten appeal.

PERFECT RATIO
See-through host chairs
and a zinc-topped
outdoor table restfully
counterbalance four mod-
pattern side seats.

LINKED MOTIFS
Natural textures and
modern-motif floral
fabrics link the great
room to the outdoors,
kitchen, and bedrooms.

Coastal color

Seaside cottage style doesn't have to mean a maritime color scheme of red, white, and blue or sea-glass green. Balance your nautical notions with a palette that suits you. Lighthearted restraint. Easy-care, durable furniture, rugs, and window treatments in colors of sand and cloud exude a casual, coastal vibe. Dress windows lightly to allow the vista to become part of your decor. Energize those neutrals with vivid pops of color and pattern as refreshing as a new beach towel. Bright and breezy. If you want to play off of a seaside feel, create your nod to the view outside with motifs such as sea creatures, shells, and botanicals, and materials such as canvas and natural wovens. New and shiny doesn't work at the beach, so feel free to bring in mismatched and old furnishings, junk treasures, and found specimens. Rejuvenate and refresh them in a coat of brightly colored paint covered with a touch of glaze to add patina. If you're looking for paint inspiration, find a host of projects to update your furnishings at *BHG.com/paintprojects*.

Color clue

Painting a ceiling a warm color visually lowers the height and adds coziness.

CONTEMPORARY COTTAGE

Yellow shines brightly in the kitchen where white-painted cabinets and beaded board take a turn toward contemporary, thanks to the progressively profiled plastic stools and stainless-steel countertops and appliances, which reference steely gray surfaces displayed throughout the home.

CAPTURE COOL

above left **A flokati rug** anchors a fab furniture arrangement of orange patent-leather chairs and an acrylic coffee table.

SYNCHRONIZE ELEMENTS

above middle **Orange and** browns reappear as artwork and bedding in the guest room. Shell chandeliers, the lattice duvet, and a cowhide bench echo colors and images outfitting the living areas.

ADD PUNCH

above right **A perky** shower curtain and tub toys carry the playful palette into the kids' bathroom.

OPTIMIZE PANACHE

right **One coverlet and** three pillows saturate this otherwise-neutral bedroom with color. Zebra prints and woolly goat-hair chairs contribute a collected and textural character.

"This design is all about bringing in threads of color, vintage pieces, and whimsical motifs and anchoring them with neutrals."

—**Tara Seawright,** interior designer

make the transition

cohesive composition

Harmonious hues inspired by ocean vistas ebb and flow to link the comfortable family-centered spaces of this La Jolla, California, home.

Shifting from pale to saturated, the sea blues and greens, whitecap whites, and beachy tones that cover walls and furnishings carry the eye through living and sleeping quarters to entertaining and work spaces. Follow these same strategies for choosing and using color to create your own pleasing transitions.

Find a muse. Collect magazine images of adjoining rooms sporting different wall colors and/or design palettes. Note color connections that appeal to you. Or take inspiration from a fabulous fabric pattern.

Vary the carry-through. Segue from room to room with subtle shifts in color. A careful progression can take you to an entirely different hue without experiencing a startling change. Neutral tones should shift room-to-room as well.

Create consistent contrast. Paint every bit of woodwork bright white to fashion repeating frameworks that highlight deeper wall and ceiling colors.

TONAL QUALITIES
Aquamarine deepens on walls, pales on upholstery fabric, and repeats in pillows, curtain panels, and accents.

Select furniture, textiles, finishes, and accessories that further your color scheme and smooth the juxtapositions of palettes from room to room.

A STUDY IN COLOR
left Wearing the same curtain fabric and white-painted cabinetry, the cream-walled craft room is solidly allied with the adjacent family room. Apple green pulled from the room's inspiring drapery fabric reappears here in the rug, desktop accessories, and chairs.

STACKED INTEREST
above left Wainscot gracefully anchors walls covered in greenish-blue grass cloth—the color darkens on the front door to complement the family room walls. A flower-pattern area rug previews botanical motifs and sand and surf shades showcased in adjacent spaces.

GRAY SUITS
above Gray paint, used on the ceiling and on bookcase interiors, adds another color to the mix. The ceiling's grayish tone (see page 202) softens the transition between walls and white ceiling beams. The foggy hue also breaks up the bookcases' vast whiteness and highlights collections.

ROLE REVERSAL

above **Present a dominant hue in a supporting role, but repeat ceiling treatments to underscore a spatial relationship.** In the dining room, aqua gives way to walls covered in golden grass cloth, while cream ceilings match those in the foyer.

PRIMARY COMBO

right **Choose a duo-tone fabric pattern that combines two of your palette's primary hues to create a lovely link between flanking rooms.**

BONDING TEXTURES

far right **Though the grass-cloth coverings in foyer and dining room differ in hue, they forge a tactile, visual, and style-apt bond.**

WARM INFUSION

opposite **Chocolate-hue upholstery fabric, bronze cabinet hardware, and espresso finishes on wood link to toasty shades seen elsewhere in the home, adding warm contrast to the cabinetry.**

SPOTLIGHT WHITES

above left **Cream walls and ceilings allow white woodwork to step forward instead of blending in.**

GO GREEN

above right **Introducing greens tending toward yellow gives the kitchen its own identity without jarring. The cheery color pulled from the geometric drapery fabric brightens chairs and cabinet interiors. The vibrant citrusy hue carries through the room's midpoint, finishing the expansive island in an arresting acid green.**

Giving weight to molding

Should moldings be enhanced or hidden? That depends on what role they play in your room's decor. Rule of thumb. If your moldings are wide or prominent decorative elements that deserve extra attention, or they surround architectural features you'd like to emphasize, paint them a color that contrasts with the walls. If they are nondescript, make them disappear by painting them the same color as the walls, but in a glossier finish. Add some detail. If you want to give your ceilings a more prominent role, moldings can help raise the eye on your walls. Attach strips of molding several inches below the crown molding and fill in the space with a special wall treatment. Or attach a frame of molding to the ceiling several inches inside the edge of the room; paint the frame and crown molding a color that contrasts with the wall, and paint the ceiling space between the two moldings a third color.

COLORFUL SILHOUETTE
Repeat chocolatey wood tones with dark upholstered furniture that stands out against white tile.

Color clue
Use mirrored surfaces on walls, furnishings, and accents to bounce color around a room.

BATHING BEAUTIES

above **Dress tub decks with colorfully packaged amenities; outfit tub-side windows with fabric shades that can be pulled to heighten privacy.**

FINE FINISH

above middle **Introduce color using towels, soap dispensers, area rugs, and shower curtains. Add white knobs to dark-finished cabinets for contrast.**

LOVELY LINKS

top right **A banded pillow brings the dining room's golden tones to the master bedroom; ceramic vessels and blooms reference the brighter greens appearing in the craft room and kitchen.**

SERENE SHIFT

above right **Brighter greens from communal rooms shade to soothing sage in the master bedroom. The herbal hue appears in the comforter, which also ties to the bath's silvery gray.**

Make tranquil spaces more attractive by suspending sparkling chandeliers, hanging dazzling draperies, and introducing flickers of metallic shimmer.

open up

color connected

Where to start and stop wall colors is only one of the challenges posed by an open floor plan. See how this family solved their palette puzzle in a creative way.

In this New England seaside open-plan home, cottage colors and a summerhouse theme create perfect harmonies that flow from room to room. You, too, can forge strong and lively color connections by:

Considering the whole picture. Look carefully at sight lines from different sides of the room to determine where to showcase or shift colors within the space. Taking digital snapshots can help you see in 2D where colors will attract and draw the eye.

Going for flow. Create cohesion by carrying the same neutral backdrops—such as white walls and ceilings, painted or stained woodwork, and hardwood flooring or carpeting—from one area to the next.

Transitioning sensibly. Shift wall colors at architectural stopping/starting points, like corners, but use the same trim color throughout a space as the tie that binds.

Boldly bonding. Use a vibrant hue or an accent wall color to direct attention from one room to the next. Vary the amount and shades of your color in different areas.

FABRICS & FINISHES
Light wood finishes and strategically placed red fabrics carry attention to lipstick-red walls, defining the kitchen and neighboring seating area.

SAY IT AGAIN
Though red is used as the primary hue throughout this media room off the kitchen, it takes on a smaller role as piping on a pair of wing-backs.

CREATE BOUNDARIES

above **Switch wall colors to divvy up floor space and define functional areas in a grandly proportioned great room. While red walls endow the kitchen core with its own identity, substantial white walls in the living room reiterate the kitchen cabinets' color story. Red makes its splash in this space in cheery cushions and pillows.**

COLOR RULES

right **Distribute color artistically in an open-plan home. Once you pick a dominant color that you want to pop throughout, display it at least three times in a single room or in viewed-together spaces. Use it on a wall or walls, in patterned upholstery fabric, in artwork, and in small accents. Break up endless walls with a bookcase, shelving, window seat, or decorative screen.**

PLAY WITH PATTERN

opposite **Arrange** energetically patterned textiles that share a palette as noteworthy exclamation points. When it comes to making an impact in large open rooms, more is always more and bigger is better. Mass piles of pillows and lay down large area rugs with plenty of panache.

COMPLETE SUMMARY

above **Vividly striped** runners in the kitchen and the great-room contain all the hues used in the open living areas. In both cases, the rugs are laid in spaces that are otherwise relatively quiet in color. A repeated object or textile that summarizes your palette is ideal for keeping your look pulled together and is your best jumping-off point for building a cohesive color scheme.

BLUR BORDERS

above right **Coordinate** contiguous spaces using architectural embellishments and a common color. Gold grass cloth brightens the molding-paneled foyer and stairway walls and repeats, sans molding, to link lower and upper hallways. The wide decorative trim references the living room's shiplap-sided walls and the kitchen's paneled ceiling and beaded-board accents. The sunny gold tone pops up in area rugs and fabrics used throughout the home.

Use a color progression

Subtly modify your color palette as you move from communal spaces into personal retreats. Utilize toned-down versions of your living area's brightest shades to fashion serene sanctuaries that stay in sync with the rest of your home. Keep it in neutral. The easiest way to fashion a whole-house palette is to keep major furnishings and architectural finishings in neutral hues. Employ the same trim color in all rooms. Update old seating with slipcovers to make it work with your new scheme. Keep it in proportion. For an easy room-to-room transition, use all the same hues throughout your home and vary the proportions in each room. Use one hue as a wall color in one room and as an accent color in the next.

PRETTY IN PINK
opposite top **The lipstick red from the living areas lightens to pink in the master bedroom. Crisp white slipcovers and touches of gold further the connection.**

WHITE BALANCE
opposite bottom **In the bath, snowy textiles and fittings spotlight a focal wall covered in pink lattice wallpaper.**

SEASONAL SHADES
this photo **Change accents such as the pillow to add springtime tones and motifs that refresh and enliven the pink boudoir.**

color workroom

Use our hands-on primer to get the basics on color relationships, painting advice from the pros, pattern lessons, and more.

"Any color palette or
combination that exists in
nature—a landscape,
a flower, or a fruit—will work
perfectly for you. Voilà!
Now you are a color pro!"

—Elaine Griffin, interior designer

color 101

If your drab, tired rooms have finally worn out their welcome and you're ready for a change, read this primer on waking up your rooms with color.

We love color. **BUT COLOR CAN BE COMPLEX.** Although it's easy to ooh and ahh over photos of gorgeous homes in books or magazines, yearning to refresh and personalize your own house, you have no idea how to duplicate that mood or design yourself. **FOLLOW OUR COLOR GUIDE.** This chapter takes the mystery and fear out of choosing and using color. It includes a crash course in color theory (without the art-professor speak), definitions for several key terms you're sure to run across, a few Web resources, and a walking tour of nine approaches to inviting color into a room, from subtle and safe to dynamic and daring. **LEARN WHAT IMPACTS COLOR.** In addition, we offer insights on lighting a room—the right lighting changes EVERYTHING—and introducing pattern into your decor. (Trust us: It's not nearly as intimidating as you might think.) Plus, we run down the basic procedure for the perfect paint job, the right tools to use, and advice from the pros. **USE YOUR NEWFOUND WISDOM.** Of course we've included photos and stunning illustrations to show you exactly what we mean when we're talking about a split-complementary scheme or a color's saturation. We're confident that at least one approach—maybe more!—will speak to you as the right way to bring creative color into your home. So sharpen your pencils and get ready to let your creative juices flow, because the lessons start now.

The greatest invention in history (for decorating purposes, anyway) is the wheel—the color wheel. Here's how to use this artistic wonder.

Color originates in light. Isaac Newton (1642–1727) discovered that light refracted through a crystal prism results in the colors of the rainbow. When Newton took his color spectrum and imagined it as a circle, he created the very useful color wheel tool. By this simple act, Newton made color relationships easier to see. A color wheel is made of 12 hues: three primary colors, three secondaries, and six tertiaries. Color relationships (see the images, *opposite*) based on these groups form the basis of color theory.

Color in harmony. As you create a color scheme for your room, keep in mind that everything is about balance. Color harmony in any palette is achieved through dominance (how much any color is used within a space), recurrence (how often it is used), and placement (where it's used).

ONLINE RESOURCES

BHG.com. Play with palettes and change them with a click of the mouse.

colormatters.com. This site discusses the symbolism of color, how to design with it, and how our eyes see color.

colorsontheweb.com. This site offers inspiration and tools for designing your own color scheme. The Color Wizard automatically provides accent hues to go with your chosen color.

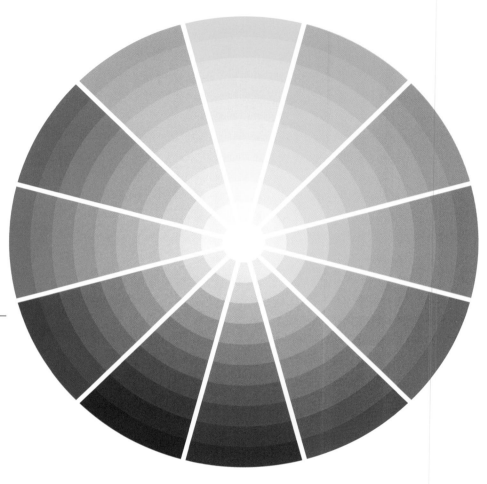

COLOR TERMS

Primary colors
Pure colors—red, yellow, and blue—that combine to create all the other colors.

Secondary colors
Colors that result from a combination of equal parts of two primary colors—green, orange, and purple.

Tertiary colors
Colors resulting from an equal mix of one primary and one secondary color; examples are blue-green and red-purple.

Neutrals
Colors that are neither warm nor cool. Examples include white, black, and gray.

Tint
Color made lighter by adding white to it. Pink is a tint of red, for example.

Shade
A color made darker by adding black to it. Navy blue is a shade of blue. Shade also refers to slight variations in a color.

Saturation
The degree of a color's purity in relation to gray. Saturated colors are clear and contain no gray. Think fire-engine red and lemon yellow.

Value
The brightness of a color. The higher the value, the more light a color emits.

Opacity
The amount of light that passes through a color. If light passes through completely, the color is transparent or clear. If light is muted or partially blocked, the color is translucent. If light is blocked completely, the color is considered opaque.

MONOCHROMATIC

Such a scheme starts with a single color—in the case of this kitchen, a quiet sage green. To enliven a monochromatic scheme, incorporate tints and shades of your chosen color in solids and patterns. Toss in some texture for additional depth and interest.

ANALOGOUS

These colors sit next to each other on the color wheel; they offer enough variety to spice up a room but still manage to play nicely together. Here, a melange of blue tints and shades cluster with greens and yellows.

COMPLEMENTARY

Colors residing on opposite sides of the color wheel absolutely attract—attention. Note how the green walls and ottomans positively burst to life against raspberry red pillows and flowers.

SPLIT COMPLEMENTARY

In this scheme, a color and the colors analogous to its complement are combined for a high degree of contrast that's not quite as intense as a true complementary scheme. The pink dresser, blue-green chair, and yellow-green wallpaper are somewhat more subdued than, say, brilliant red and green.

TRIAD

Triad colors are three hues equidistant on the color wheel, such as the red, yellow, and blue in this family room. Such a combo yields a colorful and vibrant yet balanced scheme.

TERTIARY

Tamer than a triad palette, these colors result from the mix of a primary and a secondary color. This bedroom, for example, makes use of yellow-green and blue-green with white for visual balance.

color 101 | monochromatic

A single hue—mysterious aubergine—
for a room provides a lively palette with
the addition of shades, tints, and neutrals.

at the windows
Off-white linen punctuated
with purple embroidered
starbursts dresses the
windows but still appears airy.

deck the wall
Ivory painted beaded-
board wainscoting
lightens the look, while
quiet lavender coats
the wall above.

small touch
A purple-and-white
tweed cloaks the
ottoman, giving a
hint of texture and
pattern in front of
the solid-color sofa.

big blinds
Pleated shades in
semi-sheer off-
white fabric filter
harsh sun without
blocking light.

flower power
This large-scale
floral on a white
background adds
variety and interest
to the sofa and small
printed pillows.

layer on color
A white industrial-
grade carpet makes
a uniformly soft
flooring surface.
Dress it up with a
patterned rug in
purple and ivory.

pillow punctuation
Tufted with purple
buttons, this small-
pattern pillow in
purple and ivory
provides dimension
against the purple
backdrop of the sofa.

deep purple
Slubby and nubby
aubergine fabric covers
the sofa with rich color
and texture, anchoring
the room.

catch the wave
Shades of purple, white,
and olive undulate
across the chair,
creating an
energetic vibe.

Why this room works

As you can see from this illustration, a one-color scheme can indeed pack a punch. Here's how we got the most mileage out of a single hue.

Call for backup.
An all-purple room would have been overwhelming to the eye, so we tapped an old friend—ivory—for assistance. This clean, bright neutral lightened the walls and windows and offered a bright break from the deep purples elsewhere.

Step up the paint chip.
To usher variety—but not other colors—into the room, we slid a notch or two up the paint card. Paint chips are organized so that all colors on the card have the same color value (that is, the amount of pigment); the lighter colors simply have more white added to them. Including these tints means that the colors won't clash but there will still be some variety in the scheme.

Pile on patterns.
Inviting patterns of all scales and motifs into the room—while staying within the purple palette—gives the eye something to delight in, something to examine. Patterns energize and enliven a space.

PLUM BEAUTIFUL
Just one hue—purple, in this case—doesn't mean boring or bland when you invite fabrics with different textures and patterns. Using neutral whites and ivories expands decorating options without veering outside the scheme.

color 101 | analogous

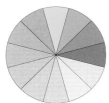

Widen the field of choices by choosing a hue and including its nearby neighbors to flavor your room.

all-out pattern
Pattern climbs the walls in statement-making curtain panels. The interlocking geometric print brings energy to the room.

felt so good
Tangy orange felt stitched into a pillow and ringed with hot pink ruffles softens the yellow armchair.

crinkled pink
Shades in lipstick pink pick up the rosy hue from the flanking curtains and provide touch-me texture.

juicy hues
Thick upholstery in a geometric orange-and-pink print energizes the ottoman and repeats hues elsewhere in the room.

go for the gold
Gold-yellow silk faille, a subtle ridged weave, gives the sofa light texture and an air of formality.

deep impact
Magenta with white embroidered flowers adds airy pattern to accent pillows.

gilded age
A gold-tone flat-woven fabric covers the armchair for a coordinating, but not matched, look with the sofa.

a touch of sun
The palest buttercream color graces the walls, creating a quiet pastel background for the more strident hues.

understated underfoot
Blond wood is a warm-leaning but neutral base for the saturated colors.

pink pair
Deep pink printed flowers play off the embroidered pillow pattern. Buttons and a silk flower add zing.

Why this room works

Casting a wider net to catch a few colors for a room yields more shades and tints to choose from and a more dynamic mood. Here's how we pulled this decor together with three analogous hues.

Staying solid.
Three large elements—the walls, armchair, and sofa—shimmer in similar golden hues without pattern and with very little texture. This yellow is treated almost as a neutral, grounding the room with a solid, sturdy background for brighter, bolder accents.

One wild, eye-catching print.
With so many hot hues sizzling in the room, a shot of white at the window—gridded with a mod geometric print of orange and pink—commands attention. As vivid as this fabric is, it demonstrates restraint in displaying only two of the room's main colors.

Pair orange and red.
With golden-yellow as the anchor, its color-wheel neighbors throw in a few punches on the window shades, throw pillows, ottoman, and wide-stripe rug.

SUPER SATURATED STYLE
Packed with punchy colors and vibrant patterns, this analogous scheme leans on a trio of hues: yellow, orange, and red, supplemented with tints in pale yellow and bright pink.

color 101 | complementary

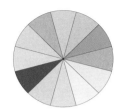

Opposites do indeed attract when they're brought into the same room. See how they play off each other with effervescence and delight.

brilliant blossoms
Bright orange blooms on an aqua ground bring a splash of large-scale pattern at the windows.

white done right
The subtle texture of white matelassé adds tone-on-tone pattern and depth to the sofa.

slim lines
Skinny stripes on a pillow bring green into the palette and linear geometry to the mix.

nubby surface
Woven ivory shades create a plane of neutral texture over the windows.

classic combo
A busy white-on-orange pattern brings energy to the classically styled and tufted ottoman.

bold blue
Azure fabric adds saturated color that plays off the pale blue walls and provides a solid accent amid the patterned pillows on the sofa.

walk the planks
Distressed wood flooring washed in blue stain creates a rustic contrast to the smooth leather and tone-on-tone matelassé pattern of the large furniture pieces.

dazzling damask
Classic pattern in a brilliant color fusion makes a playful statement on the white sofa.

sleek and smooth
Ivory leather, with its smooth surface and subtle sheen, enlivens the armchair.

walls with wow
Though it has the texture of hand-troweled plaster, the walls are covered with plaster-coated paper.

Why this room works

Orange and blue may sit across from each other on the color wheel, but they look completely at home next to each other in this setting. That's because they vibrate with energy and inject the room with verve. Here's how we introduced these opposites with such success.

Neutral furniture. Big, pricey pieces, including the chair and couch, stayed in the neutral zone of white and just-off-white. Draining them of color freed us to plunk down pattern and punch with ottoman, pillows, curtains, and colors on the walls and floors.

Orange accent. Arguably the brighter and stronger of the two colors, orange was kept on a leash so that it made a statement without screaming for attention. Building additional blue into the scheme makes it more livable for most folks.

Restrained pattern. Furnishings, floors, and walls are more or less solid in hue; pattern appears on the ottoman, on pillows, and in the curtains only. Confining pattern to just a few places quiets a potentially loud palette.

WHAT A COMPLEMENT!
White furnishings dashed with orange-and-blue fabrics and accents wake up this room like a morning pot of coffee. Blue walls and floors take the hot edge off the orange touches.

color 101 | split complementary

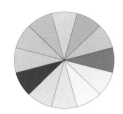

Somewhat less high-contrast than a straight-up complementary color scheme, the split complementary offers energy without exhaustion.

hint of tint
Pale yellow fabric upholsters the sofa for an almost-neutral appearance.

whitewalls
Nubby grass cloth in bleached white covers the walls with texture and a tropical feel.

tweed coat
Loosely woven coral-on-yellow fabric covers the armchair for a dose of warmth and soft texture.

blurry blue
A small-scale print in cloudy blue ovals tempers the boldness of the blue rug and large-scale drapery fabric.

bright blossoms
A busy floral window treatment fabric provides the inspiration for this enchanting color scheme.

shades of light
White matchstick blinds bring pale texture to the window. The loose weave allows in ample light.

by the beach
Whitewashed plank flooring resembles distressed wood, giving the room a carefree cottage vibe.

burst of color
A circular starburst pattern enlivens the ottoman. Juicy color contrasts with the distressed wood legs.

fruity fun
Melon-hue paint juices up storage boxes under the ottoman for a splash of solid color.

Why this room works

A bit quieter and more balanced than its complementary cousin, the split-complementary scheme incorporates hues that are near-opposites for a more even-mannered mood. Here's how these hues came together so cooperatively.

The white elements have texture. What could have been flat, ho-hum facets of this room—the walls and floors—instead boast subtle but interesting texture, which plays with light and tantalizes the senses. These parts prevent the room from feeling flat and one-dimensional.

Two shades of blue make an appearance. While the other two colors, melon and pale yellow, stay true to form throughout, both light aqua and royal blue star in this show, giving it both a breezy and a bold quality.

A STEP BACK
A giant rug bursting with yellow circles sets a colorful stage for this space and strikes a balance with the coral and mellow yellow furnishings.

color 101 | triad

Nearly exploding with vibrant color, the triad approach incorporates three colors equidistant from each other on the color wheel. Good-bye, yawning. Hello, energy!

caramel color
Burnt-orange walls dramatically warm the space and make it feel close and cozy.

ivory accent
Cream-colored paint coats the window trim and casing to delineate it from the walls.

a touch of shine
For extra pizzazz, ethereal olive green organza can impart a subtle shimmer as a skirt on the curtain panels.

tropical paradise
A floral print of plum, brown, green, orange, yellow, and pink brings in large-scale pattern and encapsulates the color palette.

green with envy
Olive green silk pillows take the hue to the purple sofa, helping to blend the intense seating with the rest of the room.

simple shades
Rustic rattan shades shield the room from bright sunlight and usher in another natural element.

regal seat
Brilliant purple upholstery packs a wallop on the sofa, ensuring that the violet leg of the triad is well represented.

check it out
A tiny checked print is about all the additional pattern this room needs. Use it to refresh pillows on the sofa.

quirky cork
Cushy sheets of cork warm the floor; it wears like wood but has more visual texture.

show some skin
Almost-matte, soft green leather sheathes a trio of ottomans, an earthy complement to their woven bases.

Why this room works

The three secondary colors—green, orange, and purple—join forces in this breezy getaway of a room, amping up the color intensity and welcoming nature inside. Here's how these very different hues work so well together.

Similar saturations. Though there's a bit of variation in the colors (two shades of green, for example), everything else possesses like intensity. That is, there's nary a pastel or clear, juicy hue among them. The green, orange, and purple have been muted somewhat by the addition of black, so they all have a slight smokiness that keeps them at the same saturation.

Solid ground. Because tans and browns occur so often in nature (dry grass, bare soil, etc.), they coexist peacefully with almost every color. Here, cork flooring, rattan blinds, and woven wood ottomans give the striking scheme good grounding.

NATURAL BEAUTY
Warm, welcoming, and a touch tropical, this living room feels like a barefoot paradise, thanks to hues and materials borrowed from nature: green fabrics, cork flooring, floral-pattern curtains, and woven blinds.

color 101 | tertiary

Three colors in the same neighborhood gather for a charming get-together where all three share the spotlight and enjoy each other's company.

beautiful bordeaux
Wine-color silk drips with drama as a slouchy, seductive accent pillow.

window wonder
Dark brown wooden blinds provide subtle pattern and contrast with the beige walls and trim.

color wheels
A busy ethnic print injects a dose of small-scale pattern to balance the only other overt pattern in the room—the large rose motif.

liquid silk
Cobalt blue silk has just the right hand and drape for dreamy curtains that bring rich bands of color to the room.

coming up roses
Three shades of blue sketch out a large rose blossom on a flax-color ground. It shares a shade of turquoise with the red-violet pillow pattern.

sturdy walls
Stone-color paint draws the walls to the warm side of neutral.

on solid ground
Medium-tone wood planks cover the floor with a traditionally neutral base.

sumptuous and smooth
Soft brown leather is stretched over the armchair and sofa for a no-fuss yet beckoning background.

a rose is a rose
Red-violet inserts a warm tone amid the blues, creating a color bridge between the beige and cool hues.

Why this room works

Blue is the thread that weaves between all three colors in this room, so they have quite a bit of common ground. Here's how we kept the room lively but not exhausting.

Playing with scale.
We employed two fabrics with the same large pattern, a hand-painted rose and leaves, but used them on relatively small elements: a pair of throw pillows. Then we separated the pillows, placing one on the chair and the other some distance away on the sofa. What could have been easy-to-overlook accessories now burst with life because the rose motif takes center stage.

Curtain calls.
A languid river of deep blue silk pours from the curtain rod nearly to the floor—how can you look anywhere else? But once you do pull your eyes from those brilliant curtains, you notice the hue elsewhere, then the other colors, and the whole room comes into focus. These statement window dressings draw the viewer in to hear what else the space has to say.

NEUTRAL RELIEF
Because blue-violet, blue-green, and red-violet carry some tension between them, most of the room is cast in warm browns and beige. Our three tertiary hues bring clear, saturated color to the curtains, accents, and pillows.

color 101 | neutrals

Some folks might equate neutral with boring, but as this palette proves, that certainly doesn't have to be the case.

snow leopard
A muted animal print in pale gray and white brings a touch of the exotic to a throw pillow.

cloudy days
White quatrefoils march in unison across gray wallpaper to give the walls dimension and interest.

a hint of glint
Shimmery silver silk sweeps along either side of the window; the tailored cornice outlined in black adds a touch of masculinity to the room.

not-so-bland beige
Linen-textured beige fabric upholsters the sofa, warming the room somewhat and picking up a hue from the striped armchair.

drop over
Teardrops in beige and gray cover the surface of the round ottoman and mimic the shapes on the rug below.

fluid movement
Like organic tentacles, the white pattern on gray fabric fashions an undulating rhythm for accent pillows on the solid sofa.

shades of gray
Beige and shades of gray stripe the chair in a linear pattern, creating a contrast with the many rounded patterns.

throw a curve
The swirling designs on the gray-and-white rug bring energetic movement to the room.

Why this room works

Neutrals are often the scheme of choice because they are hard to mess up—but neutrals can also teeter into tedium. Here's how we kept our room awake and energized.

Eye-popping pattern. Within a restrained palette, pattern increases exponentially in importance. In our room, a hypnotically swirling rug design catches attention, as does a playfully striped chair. Even the wallpaper, which is a relatively restrained geometric, radiates with rhythm.

Doses of black. Few colors, even saturated ones, imbue a room with as much drama and weight as strategic dabs of black. Note how black banding on the curtains and cornice clearly defines both so neither gets lost amid a sea of gray. The armchair, too, gains a certain gravitas with a black upholstered back.

BLAND-BANISHING NEUTRALS
A grouping of grays teams up with white, black, and a handful of beiges in this surprisingly dynamic neutral room. A fistful of fabrics—with a harmony of different sheens and patterns—elevates everything in the mix.

color 101 | warm

Reminiscent of fire and sunshine, the warm side of the color wheel produces a palette that will infuse your home with coziness year-round.

saucy stripes
Striped pillows in rich bronze, olive green, and crimson provide visual contrast and enliven the solid shapes.

tangy treat
Button tufting adds dimension to a pillow in olive green silk.

fringe on top
Playful tassel trim in gold and burgundy dances along the traditional swagged valance at the windows.

in the red
Burgundy chenille, a sumptuous choice for both the eyes and the hands, softens the straight lines of the sofa.

cozy combo
Warm ivory and toasty beige bring neutral hues to the window trim and the walls.

hothouse flowers
Olive green washes the background of this dynamic floral, injecting a touch of coolness into the hot-hue pattern.

yellow jacket
Mustard-yellow leather upholstery for the side chair creates a zesty counterpoint to the burgundy sofa.

clean slate
Mottled slate tile, a natural beauty, covers the floor. Though warm in tone, it's cool on the feet.

Why this room works

Interior designers have long employed warm colors—red, orange, and yellow—to take the chill off of an east- or north-facing room or a space without windows. Here's how these hues heat up this decor without scorching it.

Olive green is a counterpoint.
Granted, pure green is a cool color, but adding yellow (a warm hue) to create an olive cast provides a striking, unexpected accent hue in this glowing space. (Consider, for example, how different the room would look with orange as an accent.)

Walls are warm but not hot.
Toasty beige certainly falls on the warm side of the spectrum, but it has neutralizing tendencies because it contains some gray. Coating the walls with this hue goes a long way toward tempering the room's heat.

FIERY SUNSET
Just as the sun heats up the earth with its golden rays, warm hues—mustard yellow, olive green, and rich red—make a room radiant. Natural tones (in a wood coffee table and woven baskets) add even more coziness.

color 101 | cool

Like an ocean breeze or a walk in the woods, combing the color wheel's cool colors can refresh and revive a room.

into the deep
Azure blue wall paint is deeper and darker than sky blue, bringing an almost oceany depth into the space.

clean and bright
White fabric covers the sofa, imparting a summery, porchlike feeling.

teasing touch
Crinkled fabric in sky blue introduces yet another shade of this cool hue into the grouping of pillows on the sofa.

color in the lines
A striped rug, pillow fabric, and trim add linear pattern to the mix of curvaceous patterns and forms.

pillow jewelry
Beaded sea-glass fringe dresses up an otherwise plain accent pillow.

gracious green
Green striated fabric stretches over the ottoman and a throw pillow and highlights the green in the other fabrics.

blue accents
Solid-blue fabric steps up as sharp piping on the sofa to delineate its silhouette. The fabric repeats on pillows.

cheery texture
Leaf-green pom-pom fringe adds texture and movement on the edges of an accent pillow.

all abuzz
Embroidered dragonflies add visual interest to airy white cotton lawn curtain panels.

sun screen
White textured shades provide a light transition between the cool room and the bright sun.

tropical breeze
Oversize palm fronds and flowers wave on this grand fabric; it's an attention-grabbing cover for the armchair.

Why this room works

It's easy to look at this cool-hue living space and immediately think of the beach, a kick-back porch, or a cottage with the windows open and the breezes blowing. Blues and greens tend to take the edge off a room and fill us with a sense of calm. Here's how this cool room came together.

Abundant amounts of white.
As a neutral, white furniture and fabrics are a crisp background for any colors, and blue stripes, green pillows, and cobalt walls flash like neon signs against their white neighbors. This neutral also considerably lightens the decor and bounces sunshine around the room so it doesn't appear chilly.

Greens with a drop of yellow.
Imagine how different this room would look with a kelly green ottoman and pillows—it would cool off considerably (and possibly uncomfortably). But just a hint of warm yellow in the room's greenery takes the chill out of the scheme while remaining refreshing.

CALM, COOL, AND COLLECTED
Splashed with stripes, flowers, and fun trims in blues and greens, this room is reminiscent of the seaside. White plank flooring furthers the casual, summery feeling.

color and light

Color is a product of light, so how you illuminate a room has a dramatic effect on its palette.

Light is a tricky ally when it comes to color in your home. When choosing colors, daylight is the ideal source. Natural sunlight provides a neutral balance between the warm (yellow) and cool (blue) ends of the light spectrum. But daylight isn't consistent. Northern light is cooler, while light in southern climes is the most intense. If you paint a room with a southern exposure and one with a northern exposure the same color, that color will look different in each room. Daylight also changes throughout the day and when skies are overcast.

All artificial light is not created equal either. Different types of bulbs (see below) cast slightly different light color, which in turn varies the tint of colors in your room. In addition, directional lighting (track, wall wash, uplights, accent) will also cast a different light and create different shadow patterns than an overhead or table lamp.

To help you deal with this ever-changing effect, test paint colors on your wall by painting a piece of foam board and tape the swatches up on your wall.

Leave it up for a few days before you paint so you can see how the different swatches work at different times of the day and in different light conditions. Drape large swatches of your chosen fabrics over furnishings to get their measure in differing light situations, too.

Consider the times of the day when you'll be home. If a color looks really gorgeous at 10 a.m., will you actually be there to appreciate it? If you're only home in the early morning and evening, pick color that looks best at those times of the day because that's when you'll be looking at it.

All-day lighting
See how natural and artificial lighting can affect color.

1 EARLY MORNING
In the first hours of the day, mild rays from the sunrise just barely awaken the robin's egg blue walls in this east-facing room. Because the sun is still near the horizon, its golden light casts long shadows into the room.

2 MIDDAY
Sunlight grows stronger as the sun rises in the sky and enters the room at a sharper angle, so there are almost no shadows, but a harsh patch of light has settled on one chair. The bright light also illuminates the entire room—notice that the walls are a clearer blue.

3 AFTERNOON
With a lot of daytime still left, light filters through the window, but it's not direct as the sun moves to the west later in the afternoon. Hence, the space appears darker and grayer than it did earlier in the day.

4 EVENING
Once dusk settles outside, we turn to electric lights to brighten a room—and the effect is quite different from daylight. Most lightbulbs emit yellowish light further warmed by lampshades, so the room's blue walls take on a greenish tint.

LIGHTING OPTIONS

INCANDESCENT
Incandescent lamps radiate warm, yellow-tinged light, though some manufacturers include the element neodymium in the glass bulb to neutralize it (these bulbs have a bluish cast). They are dimmable, but they also heat up quickly.

COMPACT FLUORESCENT
Blessed with long life and energy efficiency, these twist-shape bulbs cast a soft white light that's brighter and whiter than incandescents. Because they contain trace amounts of mercury, they require special disposal when they reach the end of their life span.

HALOGEN
Considered by many to best mimic pure daylight, halogen lamps are incandescents with greater efficiency and longer life, thanks to their use of halogen gas inside the glass bulb. Because halogen light appears to sparkle, it's ideal for accent lighting.

LED
Light-emitting diodes have long been used in cars and flashlights and are now illuminating homes. LEDs are dimmable, but unlike incandescents, they are highly efficient, and they stay cool while providing crisp, bright light.

pattern | try this combo

Incorporating pattern into a room may be daunting at first, but the rewards far outweigh the risks. Check out our plan and give it a try.

chocolate drop
Dot the sofa with an additional pillow of dark chocolate brown; this mottled leaf print would add more texture.

baby blue
Solid color fabric in delicate light blue silk is a luminous choice for curtain panels.

a bit of bravado
Cut velvet practically vibrates with a geometric pattern, enlivening a buttoned-up sofa.

hue hints
A high-contrast stripe in white, brown, sage, blue, and pink, wrapped just on the ottoman and a sofa pillow, increases the whole room's energy.

bundle of blues
Blue fabrics, both shot through with white accents, mimic the sofa fabric, but in a smaller scale that works for pillows.

pillow jewelry
This beaded tassel adds a playful aspect to the center of an accent pillow.

throw a curve
A small-scale blue-and-white pattern balances the many linear designs in the room's fabrics, bringing curved lines to the pillows.

heavy metal
Fleur-de-lis curtain tiebacks bring a bronze element to the blue silk panels when drawn aside.

crystal clear
Tone-on-tone wallpaper incorporates a scroll pattern and faux gems that add sparkle and depth to the walls.

dark shadows
An embroidered chain enlivens a brown cornice board, which takes the dark hue up the walls.

textured footing
Rattan legs on the upholstered ottoman add a touch of texture down low.

Why this room works

Reminiscent of earth and sky, brown and blue make a classic team. But choosing two gorgeous colors is the easy part; how do you add pattern to them? Try these time-tested rules of thumb.

Limit yourself.
At least one pattern should include all the colors in your palette, such as the snazzy stripe on the ottoman. Those dashes of pink and sage are color cues for accent pieces. The other patterns contain either brown or blue (plus white). Reining in your color choices will keep a room cohesive.

Large patterns for large spaces.
The biggest-scale designs in the room are the rug and the wallpaper—in terms of square footage, the walls and floor are the largest "canvases" in the space. As a rule, assign oversize patterns to those elements that are large enough to show them off properly.

Mix the scale.
This room tingles with various-sized patterns that don't overwhelm because they are kept within the same tight color palette. At least five patterns mingle harmoniously as pillows on the sofa.

GOOD VIBRATIONS

Soulful browns and breezy blues electrify this living room, thanks to the zingy patterns throughout. A geometric fabric gives shape to the sturdy lines of the sofa, stripes dazzle and play on the ottoman, and the rug's diagonal grid anchors the whole patterned palette.

pattern | how it works

Feeling color confident? Here are daring ways to pump up the pattern in your palette.

1 PATTERN PLAY
Similar colors in this jagged-pattern rug and a wave-print chair cushion tie them together for a surprisingly cohesive combination. Note that the larger print is on the bigger surface.

2 DECK THE WALLS
Wallcoverings, whether paper or fabric, might be the fastest way to pack a room with pattern and impart shape and architecture to an otherwise bland space. Here, a standard bath breaks out of its boxy shell with organic pink-and-white paper lining the walls.

3 SMALL STEPS
Pattern shy? There are lots of low-commitment ways to pull pattern into a room: Accent pillows, a throw draped over a chair, removable slipcovers for furniture, and even wall art can up the design and dazzle. In this room, the repetition of green links the different patterns.

4 GRAYSCALE Pattern doesn't have to mean cacophonous color. In this bedroom, white and gray make a graphic statement when splashed across the walls and bed. An indigo coverlet balances a zesty yellow-green pillow and pale yellow curtains.

Color clue
A mostly neutral room needs just a punch or two of zesty color for maximum impact.

Why this room works

This bedroom boldly proclaims its propensity toward pattern and holds seemingly clashing patterns in exquisite balance. Take a lesson from this daring design.

Neutrals upfront. Gray, white, and black can hold their own as stars of the show. Plus, they are sturdy building blocks for whatever design direction you take. Here, the vines-and-flowers wallpaper has just enough of a modern bent that it's gender-neutral.

Warm and cool. An indigo coverlet with gray motifs is a deep-hue counterpoint to the white-ground wallpaper. But because gray can often read as industrial and cold (and the blue bedspread is another cool color), warm hues, such as yellow curtains, wood blinds, and yellow-green pillows, were brought in to even things out.

Take a break. In a room with so many patterns, stretches of solids are a welcome rest from the fray. The bed linens, headboard, lamp and shade, and curtain panels tamp down the busyness as solid hues.

try a color trick

Color is quite the conjuror. Use it to disguise flaws and draw attention to assets.

1 VISIT THE DARK SIDE Pale hues visually expand and calm this bedroom, making the small space look larger than it is. In the adjacent sitting room, a dark blue wall color is employed to make the space recede visually and add depth.

2 A POP OF PATTERN Pattern and color can be used to create a focal point. In a room with neutral walls, this trellis-pattern wallpaper makes an eye-catching display from shelves that might otherwise blend in with the walls.

3 ROOM WITH A VIEW In a space with no windows, such as this basement office, a botanical wallpaper stands in for a view outside. Matching the gray of the furniture, the twining motif lightens the feel of the room.

4 DEEP DRAMA A rich color in a small space used to be a no-no, but not anymore. In this hallway, deep navy in a matte finish hides imperfections in the wall and silhouettes a shapely sconce and chair. The effect is so dramatic, the small proportions of the space are imperceptible.

5 ONE SINGULAR SENSATION Create a cozy corner or visually separate part of a room by painting the wall area in a contrasting color as seen in this reading nook.

Color clue
Dark, warm wall colors help make a barely furnished room feel well appointed.

It's magic
Use these color tricks to make the most of your room's features.

Add architecture. Rooms that lack architectural character can benefit from the clever use of color. Use two contrasting hues in horizontal bands that meet at chair-rail height to mimic wainscoting.

Set your sights high. Use your ceiling's potential for dazzling design. If the walls and ceiling share the same hue, the ceiling appears taller and the space roomier. A sharp line between the walls and ceiling, whether with a drastic color change or a stretch of crown molding, clearly defines the ceiling's height.

Hello, sunshine. Consider how much natural light a room gets and what sun exposure it receives. South- and west-facing windows usher in strong sunlight, so cooler hues inside balance it. Northern and easterly exposures whisper with milder light—warm colors on walls and furnishings will take off any chill.

Color binding. Forge a visual link between rooms by using the same color on trim or carrying one accent color through every room.

painting | tools of the trade

Once you've selected your colors, it's time to roll up your sleeves! Here's a roundup of what you'll need to tackle almost any painting project in your home.

PAINTER'S TAPE
Less sticky than other tapes, it won't mar walls or molding. Use it to mask edges and trim you don't want to paint.

DROP CLOTH
This sheet of heavy cotton canvas will protect furniture and floors from dust and drips.

PUTTY KNIFE
Use its flat blade to smear surfacing compound in nail holes and gouges, then swipe the edge across to smooth.

SANDERS
Use sandpaper or a sanding block to smooth surfaces and give tooth to glossy finishes.

PAINTBRUSHES
Paint walls with a 3-inch brush. Paint trim with an angled brush. Apply latex paint with artificial bristles; alkyd with natural.

PAINT SHIELD
This plastic shield will guard any straight edge (say, a window sill or molding) from smears.

PAINT TRAY
Essential for loading up a roller with paint, the tray's gridded liner also prevents overloading the roller and dripping.

ROLLER FRAME
Slide a paint roller on this frame for easy application of paint over a large wall area.

ROLLERS
Rollers come in different naps to accommodate walls with texture. The smoothest walls are suited to the shortest nap, *left*, while heavily textured or rough walls need a thick-nap roller, *far right*.

PRIMER
To paint over raw wood, bare drywall, stained walls, or walls painted a dark or bright color, start with a coat of primer.

Paint comes in several degrees of sheen: matte, flat, satin or eggshell, semigloss, and high-gloss. Choose the finish that suits your application.

1 MATTE FINISH Rich and almost velvety-looking, matte finish reflects no light. Such a paint certainly looks dramatic, but it's difficult to clean, so it's not for high-traffic rooms or households with children.

2 FLAT FINISH One step up on the sheen scale, flat paint reflects light very subtly and can be almost chalky in appearance. Slightly easier to clean than matte paint, it's good for ceilings, offices, and bedroom walls.

3 SATIN FINISH A very popular choice for its durability and easy-cleaning, satin paint is somewhat shinier than flat paint, giving walls more dimension. Use it on the walls in rooms that get more wear and tear, such as hallways, kids' spaces, and family rooms.

4 SEMIGLOSS FINISH Semigloss paint bounces quite a bit of light around a room, giving it a dynamic appearance. Easy to clean and long-wearing, it's the sheen of choice for kitchens, bathrooms, cabinetry, and furniture. High-gloss finishes, not pictured here, are best suited to floors, stairway railings, and other applications where a hard, easy-to-clean finish is desirable. Be aware, though, that high gloss emphasizes surface imperfections.

painting | on the walls

Once you've gathered your equipment, changed into grubby clothes, and opened the windows, it's time to paint. Let's get started!

1 PREPARE THE ROOM.
Cover furnishings and floors, remove outlet covers, and tape off the baseboards and window casing. Readying the room may take twice as long as actually painting it.

2 START WITH A BRUSH.
Load a 3-inch paintbrush by dipping the bottom third of the bristles into paint, then lightly tapping them against the rim of the can so paint penetrates to the center of the brush.

3 OUTLINE THE ROOM.
Begin in a corner, at a door, or by a window, and "cut in" by applying a few inches of paint along the taped-off edges.

4 FILL IN.
In tight spaces, apply paint with a paintbrush, using short, X-shape strokes to spread paint evenly. Work from top to bottom.

5 PICK UP A ROLLER.
To cover large areas of wall, grab a roller and paint in a W shape across the wall, going back over wet paint to lay down an even coat. Regularly step back from the wall to judge your work.

6 CLEAN YOUR BRUSHES.
Fill a 5-gallon bucket about a third full of water (for latex paint; use mineral spirits for oil-base), swish the brush around, and knock it against the sides of the bucket to shake out the paint.

7 CLEAN YOUR ROLLER.
Use the curved side of a 5-in-1 painter's tool to squeeze as much paint as you can back into the can, then swish the roller in a bucket of water. Continue to run the tool against the roller to remove the watery paint.

8 STORE YOUR TOOLS.
Preserve good paintbrushes and keep their shape by wrapping in kraft paper once they're dry, securing the paper with rubber bands, and storing upright, handle down. Stand a roller upright on its end to dry before storing.

Splashy colors and clever paint techniques, such as a gridded wall design and paint-dipped table and chairs, light up this breakfast room. Choose a low-VOC paint formula to minimize odor and use an environmentally friendly product. Most paint manufacturers offer a low-VOC option.

What the pros know

These tips will help you achieve the best paint results.

Calculate quantity. Calculate the wall area of your room by multiplying the length of each wall by the height of the ceiling and add the products of each. Divide the total wall area by 400 square feet per gallon to get the quantity needed for one coat of paint in the room. For textured surfaces, divide by 300 square feet. Light colors usually need two coats, while dark colors may need three or more.

Tape it off. Apply no more than 8–10 inches of painter's tape at a time for a straight edge. Smooth the edges with a putty knife so no stray paint seeps underneath. Wait until paint is dry to the touch and remove the tape slowly at a 45-degree angle. If the tape begins to tear, run a crafts knife along the seam to loosen the tape.

Break time. When you take a break, wrap brushes and rollers in plastic bags, squeezing the air out, and seal with twist ties or rubber bands. To leave them overnight, place the sealed tools in the refrigerator.

painting | everything else

Just about anything in your home, from metal to fabric, can be transformed with the power of paint.

PAINTING ON METAL If the item is rusty, first brush or sand off any rust flakes (protect your eyes, nose, and hands first), and wipe clean. Then take the item outside and paint with short, even strokes using a spray paint formulated to inhibit rust and made specially for metal. Let dry fully.

PAINTING ON WOOD Sand raw wood, wipe it smooth, and prime to give it a proper surface for paint to grab. Previously painted or stained wood should be sanded to rough up the surface, then wiped clean. Apply paint with a brush, roller, or sprayer, letting it dry completely between coats.

PAINTING ON GLASS Find paint specially made for glass at the crafts store; it is available in translucent and opaque hues. To prepare the glass surface for paint, apply glass medium with a brush, and let dry. Then apply paint as desired. Protect the painted design with another coat of glass medium.

PAINTING ON FABRIC Use paints formulated for fabric or add textile medium to any paint to make it suitable for fabric. Place fabric on top of a protected surface to catch any paint that might soak through, then apply paint with a small brush. Let dry.

PAINTING ON CERAMIC Prepare the ceramic surface by brushing on tile medium, then apply paint. Let dry thoroughly. Protect your design with another coat of tile medium. You can also purchase paint formulated for use on ceramics and follow the manufacturer's instructions.

PAINTING ON NATURAL WOVENS Because heavily textured items, such as baskets, have many nooks and crannies and are porous, spray paint is a handy way to coat them in color. Be sure to use it outdoors for proper ventilation, and apply with short, even strokes.

FLOORING FIREWORKS
With a floor this dazzling, almost no more color is needed. Snazzy stripes invigorate this neutral dining room. Use a high-gloss paint finish for durability. Paint the ceiling a color used on the floor to unite the two planes.

What else you should know
Use these basic tips for the best paint job.

Primer is your friend. Primer seals in stains, blots out old paint, and provides a surface that paint can easily grab. It's especially important if you're applying a light color over a deep, rich one. In that case, primer can be tinted to your wall color to provide better coverage.

Trim or walls? When using a semigloss paint for trim, paint the trim first. If you accidentally get wall paint on your newly painted trim, the semigloss finish makes it easy to wipe off.

Let paint dry. Paint needs to dry for at least 24 hours before you pile your furniture back into the room to prevent smudging the walls. Allow drawers and doors ample time to cure so painted surfaces don't stick together.

Mix it up. When using two or more gallons of a paint color, mix all gallons together in a 5-gallon bucket. Called boxing, this will ensure that the color is uniform throughout the application. Boxing is particularly worthwhile if you're using a custom-mixed color.

palette design | make a plan

A cohesive plan allows rooms to coordinate while maintaining distinct personalities.

CREATE A THEME
Choosing from within a coordinated collection of colors and patterns ensures foolproof decorating. The sherbet shades gracing this dining room and living room offer a balance of soft tints and intense hues in playful patterns and restful solids. The key: Any combination of these colors and patterns works beautifully together.

CONNECT ROOMS
While colors echo between the dining and living rooms, they alternate volume. In the dining room, green shouts its presence, courtesy of a pear-tone rug and green accents in the art over the fireplace. But in the living room, pear green barely whispers as a delicate accent on mostly coral chair fabric.

Functional hues
Orange dining chair fabric in a dark solid stimulates the appetite and won't compete with patterned table presentations.

Big on botanical
Pattern is mostly absent from this dining room. If you crave just a touch, include a rug with an exuberant motif.

Balanced palette
The living room rug in a restrained coral and yellow grid maintains the equilibrium between the room's two dominant hues.

Wood highlights
Stain colors for tables in both rooms are suggested by the floor's beautiful parquet pattern.

Low-key spirit

Pretty tone-on-tone pattern brings subtle interest to the yellow curtain panels and complements the coral banding.

Soft touch

Switching from deep orange in the dining room to soft patterned coral, the chairs anchor the living room palette.

INCORPORATE SURROUNDINGS

Select colors to exaggerate your home's outstanding architectural features, such as the exceptionally large windows and the multiple wood tones of the inlaid floor. The windows bring so much of the outdoors in that the colors in the house are complemented by the colors of the greenery outside.

ADD WHITE

In this house, white plays dual roles with equal aplomb, emphasizing the architectural details, such as built-in cabinetry and gracious moldings. White also provides a neutral backdrop for vibrant fabrics and furnishings, enabling sofas and chairs to wear radiant color without overwhelming the modestly sized living room and dining room.

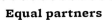

Equal partners

Yellow fabric on the sofa balances the two coral chairs, flanking a yellow painted table, and the window seat, where coral and yellow mix equally.

color sources

paint

Ace Paint
Available at Ace Hardware.
acehardware.com

Behr
Available at Home Depot.
behr.com

Benjamin Moore
Available online and at paint dealers in the U.S. and Canada. See store listings on the website.
benjaminmoore.com

Better Homes and Gardens Paint
Available across the United States at all Wal-Mart stores.
walmart.com

C2 Paint
Available at paint dealers in the U.S. and Canada. See store listings on the website.
c2paint.com

Dutch Boy
Available at paint dealers in the U.S. See store listings on the website.
dutchboy.com

Farrow & Ball
Available online and at showrooms and dealers in U.S. and Canadian metropolitan markets. See store listings on the website.
farrow-ball.com

Glidden
Available at Home Depot and Wal-Mart stores throughout the U.S.
glidden.com

Graham Paint
Available online and at select paint dealers. See store listings on the website.
grahampaint.com

Kelly-Moore Paints
Available at authorized dealers in the western and southwestern U.S. See website for store listings.
kellymoore.com

Mythic Paint
To find a Mythic Paint dealer near you, check store listings on the website.
mythicpaint.com

Olympic
Available at Lowe's.
lowes.com

Pittsburgh Paints PPG
Available at paint dealers in the U.S. and Canada. See store listings on the website.
ppgpittsburghpaints.com

Pratt & Lambert
Available at paint dealers in the U.S. and Canada. See store listings on the website.
prattandlambert.com

Ralph Lauren
Paint, wallcoverings, rugs, and fabrics available in the U.S. and Canada. See store listings on the website.
ralphlaurenhome.com

Sherwin-Williams
Available at signature stores in the U.S. and Canada. See listings on the website.
sherwin-williams.com

True Value Paint
Available in the U.S. and Canada at True Value Hardware.
truevaluepaint.com

Valspar
Available at Lowe's and paint dealers. See website for store listings.
valspar.com

YOLO Colorhouse
Available online through Home Depot and Amazon.com.
yolocolorhouse.com

wallpaper

Blue Mountain Wallcoverings
Major brands available through The Wallpaper Store at *decoratethehome.com*.
blmtn.com

Brewster Wallcoverings
Available nationwide. See website for store listings.
brewsterwallcoverings.com

Graham & Brown
Available through designers and online.
grahambrown.com

Seabrook Wallcoverings
See website for store listings.
seabrookwallpaper.com

Thibaut Wallcoverings
Wallcoverings and fabrics available through designers and retailers. See website for listings.
thibautdesign.com

Warner Wallcoverings
Available through designers and retailers. See website for listings.
warnerwalls.com

Waverly
Wallcoverings and fabrics available. See website for store listings.
waverly.com

York Wallcoverings
Available through designers and retailers. See website for listings.
yorkwall.com

fabric

Better Homes and Gardens® Home Decor Fabrics
Available at Jo-Ann Fabric and Craft Stores and online.
joann.com

Brunschwig & Fils
Fabric and wallpaper available through showrooms and interior designers.
brunschwig.com

Calico Corners
Available online and at retail locations in the U.S. See store locator on the website.
calicocorners.com

Chella Textiles
Performance fabrics available through showrooms and interior designers.
chellatextiles.com

Childress Fabrics
Retail stores in the Dallas area stock discounted designer fabrics and ship through the website.
childressfabrics.com

Duralee
Home decor fabrics available through showrooms and interior designers.
duralee.com

Fabric.com
Home decor fabrics available online at discount prices.
fabric.com

Fabric Depot
Retail store in Portland, Oregon, stocks more than 20,000 fabrics and ships internationally via website.
fabricdepot.com

Fabric Guru
Over 15,000 designer fabrics available at discount prices.
fabricguru.com

Hancock Fabrics
Home decorator fabrics available at retail locations nationwide and online.
hancockfabrics.com

House Fabric
Designer home decor fabrics and trim available online at discount prices.
housefabric.com

Jo-Ann Fabrics
Decor fabrics available at stores and online.
joann.com

Kravet
Find fabrics, trim, carpet, and furnishings through showrooms and designers.
kravet.com

Lee Jofa
Fabrics and wallpapers available through showrooms and interior designers.
leejofa.com

Osborne & Little
Fabrics and wallpapers available through showrooms and interior designers.
osborneandlittle.com

Robert Allen
Fabrics, trim, and hardware available through showrooms and designers.
robertallendesign.com

Romo Fabrics & Wallcoverings
Fabrics and wallcoverings available internationally at select showrooms. See website for listings.
romo.com

Schumacher
Fabrics, trim, furnishings, and wallcoverings available through showrooms and designers.
fschumacher.com

rugs

ABC Carpet & Home
Rugs and furnishings available at signature stores and online.
abchome.com

Angela Adams
Rugs and accessories available at select stores and online.
angelaadams.com

Capel Rugs
See website for store listings.
capelrugs.com

Chandra Rugs
Available through retailers and designer showrooms.
shopchandra.com

Company C
Rugs and furnishings available at signature stores and online.
companyc.com

Dash & Albert Rug Co.
Available at select retailers and online.
dashandalbert.com

Flor
Rugs available at select retailers and online. See website for store listings.
flor.com

Home Decorators Collection
Rugs and furnishings available online.
homedecorators.com

Liora Manne
Rugs, custom designs, fabrics, and accents available online.
lioramanne.com

Rugs USA
Rugs and furnishings available online.
rugsusa.com

Stark
Carpet, rugs, wallcoverings, and fabrics available through designers and showrooms. See website for listings. Order paint online.
starkcarpet.com

flooring

Armstrong
Laminate, linoleum, vinyl, and wood. See website for list of retailers.
armstrong.com

Duro-Design
Bamboo, cork, eucalyptus, maple, and oak. See website for list of retailers.
duro-design.com

Green Floors
Bamboo, cork, leather, linoleum, rubber, and wood. See website for list of retailers.
greenfloors.com

Lumber Liquidators
Bamboo, cork, laminate, and wood. See website for list of retailers.
lumberliquidators.com

Mannington
Hardwood, laminate, and resilient. See website for list of retailers.
mannington.com

Mohawk
Harwood, laminate, and resilient. See website for list of retailers.
mohawk-flooring.com

Natural Cork Co., Ltd.
Bamboo, cork, linoleum, and wood. See website for list of retailers.
naturalcork.com

furniture

Ballard Designs
Available at signature stores and online.
ballarddesigns.com

Better Homes and Gardens™ Furniture Collection
Available at select retailers. See website for store listings.
bhgfurniture.com

Crate & Barrel
Available at signature stores and online.
crateandbarrel.com

C.R. Laine
Available at select retailers. See website for listings.
crlaine.com

IKEA
Available at signature stores and online.
ikea.com

Lee
Available through select dealers. See website for listings.
leeindustries.com

Maine Cottage
Furniture, fabrics, accents, and paint available online.
mainecottage.com

Mitchell Gold + Bob Williams
Available through select dealers, signature stores, and online. See website for listings.
mgbwhome.com

Pearson
Available through select dealers, showrooms, and interior designers.
pearsonco.com

Pottery Barn
Available at signature stores and online.
potterybarn.com

Restoration Hardware
Available at signature stores and online.
restorationhardware.com

Room Service
Available at signature stores and online.
roomservicestore.com

West Elm
Available at signature stores and online.
westelm.com